Wonderful ways to prepare

PRESERVES

by JO ANN SHIRLEY

TITLES IN THIS SERIES

Wonderful ways to prepare

PRESERVES

PLAYMORE INC. NEW YORK USA
UNDER ARRANGEMENT WITH
WALDMAN PUBLISHING CORP.

AYERS & JAMES
SYDNEY AUSTRALIA

STAFFORD PEMBERTON PUBLISHING
KNUTSFORD UNITED KINGDOM

FIRST PUBLISHED 1979

PUBLISHED IN THE USA
BY PLAYMORE INC.
UNDER ARRANGEMENT WITH
WALDMAN PUBLISHING CORP.

PUBLISHED IN AUSTRALIA
BY AYERS & JAMES
CROWS NEST. AUSTRALIA

PUBLISHED IN THE UNITED KINGDOM
BY STAFFORD PEMBERTON PUBLISHING
KNUTSFORD CHESHIRE

COPYRIGHT © 1979
AYERS & JAMES
5 ALEXANDER STREET
CROWS NEST   N.S.W.   AUSTRALIA

ISBN 0 86908 156 X

OVEN TEMPERATURE GUIDE

Description	Gas		Electric		Mark
	C	F	C	F	
Cool	100	200	110	225	¼
Very Slow	120	250	120	250	½
Slow	150	300	150	300	1-2
Moderately slow	160	325	170	340	3
Moderate	180	350	200	400	4
Moderately hot	190	375	220	425	5-6
Hot	200	400	230	450	6-7
Very hot	230	450	250	475	8-9

LIQUID MEASURES

IMPERIAL	METRIC
1 teaspoon	5 ml
1 tablespoon	20 ml
2 fluid ounces (½ cup)	62.5 ml
4 fluid ounces (½ cup)	125 ml
8 fluid ounces (1 cup)	250 ml
1 pint (16 ounces — 2 cups)*	500 ml

* (The imperial pint is equal to 20 fluid ounces.)

SOLID MEASURES

AVOIRDUPOIS	METRIC
1 ounce	30 g
4 ounces (¼ lb)	125 g
8 ounces (½ lb)	250 g
12 ounces (¾ lb)	375 g
16 ounces (1 lb)	500 g
24 ounces (1½ lb)	750 g
32 ounces (2 lb)	1000 g (1 kg)

CUP AND SPOON REPLACEMENTS FOR OUNCES

INGREDIENT	½ oz	1 oz	2 oz	3 oz	4 oz	5 oz	6 oz	7 oz	8 oz
Almonds, ground	2 T	¼ C	½ C	¾ C	1¼ C	1⅓ C	1⅔ C	2 C	2¼ C
slivered	6 t	¼ C	½ C	¾ C	1 C	1⅓ C	1⅔ C	2 C	2¼ C
whole	2 T	¼ C	⅓ C	½ C	¾ C	1 C	1¼ C	1⅓ C	1½ C
Apples, dried whole	3 T	½ C	1 C	1⅓ C	2 C	2⅓ C	2¾ C	3⅓ C	3¾ C
Apricots, chopped	2 T	¼ C	½ C	¾ C	1 C	1¼ C	1½ C	1¾ C	2 C
whole	2 T	3 T	½ C	⅔ C	1 C	1¼ C	1⅓ C	1½ C	1¾ C
Arrowroot	1 T	2 T	⅓ C	½ C	⅔ C	¾ C	1 C	1¼ C	1⅓ C
Baking Powder	1 T	2 T	⅓ C	½ C	⅔ C	¾ C	1 C	1 C	1¼ C
Baking Soda	1 T	2 T	⅓ C	½ C	⅔ C	¾ C	1 C	1 C	1¼ C
Barley	1 T	2 T	¼ C	½ C	⅔ C	¾ C	1 C	1 C	1¼ C
Breadcrumbs, dry	2 T	¼ C	½ C	¾ C	1 C	1¼ C	1½ C	1¾ C	2 C
soft	¼ C	½ C	1 C	1½ C	2 C	2½ C	3 C	3⅔ C	4¼ C
Biscuit Crumbs	2 T	¼ C	½ C	¾ C	1¼ C	1⅓ C	1⅔ C	2 C	2¼ C
Butter	3 t	6 t	¼ C	⅓ C	½ C	⅔ C	¾ C	1 C	1 C
Cheese, grated, lightly packed,									
natural cheddar	6 t	¼ C	½ C	¾ C	1 C	1¼ C	1½ C	1¾ C	2 C
Processed cheddar	5 t	2 T	⅓ C	⅔ C	¾ C	1 C	1¼ C	1½ C	1⅔ C
Parmesan, Romano	6 t	¼ C	½ C	¾ C	1 C	1⅓ C	1⅔ C	2 C	2¼ C
Cherries, candied, chopped	1 T	2 T	⅓ C	½ C	¾ C	1 C	1 C	1⅓ C	1½ C
whole	1 T	2 T	⅓ C	½ C	⅔ C	¾ C	1 C	1¼ C	1⅓ C
Cocoa	2 T	¼ C	½ C	¾ C	1¼ C	1⅓ C	1⅔ C	2 C	2¼ C
Coconut, desiccated	2 T	⅓ C	⅔ C	1 C	1⅓ C	1⅔ C	2 C	2⅓ C	2⅔ C
shredded	⅓ C	⅔ C	1¼ C	1¾ C	2½ C	3 C	3⅔ C	4⅓ C	5 C
Cornstarch	6 t	3 T	½ C	⅔ C	1 C	1¼ C	1½ C	1⅔ C	2 C
Corn Syrup	2 t	1 T	2 T	¼ C	⅓ C	½ C	½ C	⅔ C	⅔ C
Coffee, ground	2 T	⅓ C	⅔ C	1 C	1⅓ C	1⅔ C	2 C	2⅓ C	2⅔ C
instant	3 T	½ C	1 C	1⅓ C	1¾ C	2¼ C	2⅔ C	3 C	3½ C
Cornflakes	½ C	1 C	2 C	3 C	4¼ C	5¼ C	6¼ C	7⅓ C	8⅓ C
Cream of Tartar	1 T	2 T	⅓ C	½ C	⅔ C	¾ C	1 C	1 C	1¼ C
Currants	1 T	2 T	⅓ C	⅔ C	¾ C	1 C	1¼ C	1½ C	1⅔ C
Custard Powder	6 t	3 T	½ C	⅔ C	1 C	1¼ C	1½ C	1⅔ C	2 C
Dates, chopped	1 T	2 T	⅓ C	⅔ C	¾ C	1 C	1¼ C	1½ C	1⅔ C
whole, pitted	1 T	2 T	⅓ C	½ C	¾ C	1 C	1¼ C	1⅓ C	1½ C
Figs, chopped	1 T	2 T	⅓ C	½ C	¾ C	1 C	1 C	1⅓ C	1½ C
Flour, all-purpose or cake	6 t	¼ C	½ C	¾ C	1 C	1¼ C	1½ C	1¾ C	2 C
wholemeal	6 t	3 T	½ C	⅔ C	1 C	1¼ C	1⅓ C	1⅔ C	1¾ C
Fruit, mixed	1 T	2 T	⅓ C	½ C	¾ C	1 C	1¼ C	1⅓ C	1½ C
Gelatin	5 t	2 T	⅓ C	½ C	¾ C	1 C	1 C	1¼ C	1½ C
Ginger, crystallised pieces	1 T	2 T	⅓ C	½ C	¾ C	1 C	1¼ C	1⅓ C	1½ C
ground	6 t	⅓ C	½ C	¾ C	1¼ C	1½ C	1¾ C	2 C	2¼ C
preserved, heavy syrup	1 T	2 T	⅓ C	½ C	⅔ C	¾ C	1 C	1 C	1¼ C
Glucose, liquid	2 t	1 T	2 T	¼ C	⅓ C	½ C	½ C	⅔ C	⅔ C
Haricot Beans	1 T	2 T	⅓ C	½ C	⅔ C	¾ C	1 C	1 C	1¼ C

In this table, t represents teaspoonful, T represents tablespoonful and C represents cupful.

CUP AND SPOON REPLACEMENTS FOR OUNCES (Cont.)

INGREDIENT	½ oz	1 oz	2 oz	3 oz	4 oz	5 oz	6 oz	7 oz	8 oz
Honey	2 t	1 T	2 T	¼ C	⅓ C	½ C	½ C	⅔ C	⅔ C
Jam	2 t	1 T	2 T	¼ C	⅓ C	½ C	½ C	⅔ C	¾ C
Lentils	1 T	2 T	⅓ C	½ C	⅔ C	¾ C	1 C	1 C	1¼ C
Macaroni (see pasta)									
Milk Powder, full cream	2 T	¼ C	½ C	¾ C	1¼ C	1⅓ C	1⅔ C	2 C	2¼ C
non fat	2 T	⅓ C	¾ C	1¼ C	1½ C	2 C	2⅓ C	2¾ C	3¼ C
Nutmeg	6 t	3 T	½ C	⅔ C	¾ C	1 C	1¼ C	1½ C	1⅔ C
Nuts, chopped	6 t	¼ C	½ C	¾ C	1 C	1¼ C	1½ C	1¾ C	2 C
Oatmeal	1 T	2 T	½ C	⅔ C	¾ C	1 C	1¼ C	1½ C	1⅔ C
Olives, whole	1 T	2 T	⅓ C	⅔ C	¾ C	1 C	1¼ C	1½ C	1⅔ C
sliced	1 T	2 T	⅓ C	⅔ C	¾ C	1 C	1¼ C	1½ C	1⅔ C
Pasta, short (e.g. macaroni)	1 T	2 T	⅓ C	⅔ C	¾ C	1 C	1¼ C	1½ C	1⅔ C
Peaches, dried & whole	1 T	2 T	⅓ C	⅔ C	¾ C	1 C	1¼ C	1½ C	1⅔ C
chopped	6 t	¼ C	½ C	¾ C	1 C	1¼ C	1½ C	1¾ C	2 C
Peanuts, shelled, raw, whole	1 T	2 T	⅓ C	½ C	¾ C	1 C	1¼ C	1⅓ C	1½ C
roasted	1 T	2 T	⅓ C	⅔ C	¾ C	1 C	1¼ C	1½ C	1⅔ C
Peanut Butter	3 t	6 t	3 T	⅓ C	½ C	½ C	⅔ C	¾ C	1 C
Peas, split	1 T	2 T	⅓ C	½ C	⅔ C	¾ C	1 C	1 C	1¼ C
Peel, mixed	1 T	2 T	⅓ C	½ C	¾ C	1 C	1 C	1¼ C	1½ C
Potato, powder	1 T	2 T	¼ C	⅓ C	½ C	⅔ C	¾ C	1 C	1¼ C
flakes	¼ C	½ C	1 C	1⅓ C	2 C	2⅓ C	2¾ C	3⅓ C	3¾ C
Prunes, chopped	1 T	2 T	⅓ C	½ C	⅔ C	¾ C	1 C	1¼ C	1⅓ C
whole pitted	1 T	2 T	⅓ C	½ C	⅔ C	¾ C	1 C	1 C	1¼ C
Raisins	2 T	¼ C	⅓ C	½ C	¾ C	1 C	1 C	1⅓ C	1½ C
Rice, short grain, raw	1 T	2 T	¼ C	½ C	⅔ C	¾ C	1 C	1 C	1¼ C
long grain, raw	1 T	2 T	⅓ C	½ C	¾ C	1 C	1¼ C	1⅓ C	1½ C
Rice Bubbles	⅔ C	1¼ C	2½ C	3⅔ C	5 C	6¼ C	7½ C	8¾ C	10 C
Rolled Oats	2 T	⅓ C	⅔ C	1 C	1⅓ C	1¾ C	2 C	2½ C	2¾ C
Sago	2 T	¼ C	⅓ C	½ C	¾ C	1 C	1 C	1¼ C	1½ C
Salt, common	3 t	6 t	¼ C	⅓ C	½ C	⅔ C	¾ C	1 C	1 C
Semolina	1 T	2 T	⅓ C	½ C	¾ C	1 C	1 C	1⅓ C	1½ C
Spices	6 t	3 T	¼ C	⅓ C	½ C	½ C	⅔ C	¾ C	1 C
Sugar, plain	3 t	6 t	¼ C	⅓ C	½ C	⅔ C	¾ C	1 C	1 C
confectioners'	1 T	2 T	⅓ C	½ C	¾ C	1 C	1 C	1¼ C	1½ C
moist brown	1 T	2 T	⅓ C	½ C	¾ C	1 C	1 C	1⅓ C	1½ C
Tapioca	1 T	2 T	⅓ C	½ C	⅔ C	¾ C	1 C	1¼ C	1⅓ C
Treacle	2 t	1 T	2 T	¼ C	⅓ C	½ C	½ C	⅔ C	⅔ C
Walnuts, chopped	2 T	¼ C	½ C	¾ C	1 C	1¼ C	1½ C	1¾ C	2 C
halved	2 T	⅓ C	⅔ C	1 C	1¼ C	1½ C	1¾ C	2¼ C	2½ C
Yeast, dried	6 t	3 T	½ C	⅔ C	1 C	1¼ C	1⅓ C	1⅔ C	1¾ C
compressed	3 t	6 t	3 T	⅓ C	½ C	½ C	⅔ C	¾ C	1 C

In this table, t represents teaspoonful, T represents tablespoonful and C represents cupful.

Contents

Fruits

General Hints

Equipment:

Two types of jars:
1. Spring-clip — has a rubber ring and glass lid and a spring clip to hold the lid down.
2. Screw band — has a lacquered metal disc lid with rubber band attached and a screw band to secure the disc.

Both types of jars are suitable for preserving and bottling fruit but they must be the genuine preserving jars, able to withstand boiling.

When using the glass spring-clip type of jar, new rubber rings should always be used.

Rubber rings, disc tops and screw bands should be scalded in boiling water before using. They should then be left in the boiled water until used.

Jars should be washed in hot soapy water, rinsed well and then scalded in boiling water. Do not dry. Put upside down on a rack and allow to drain. It is easier to pack fruit in wet jars than dry ones.

Jars must not be chipped or cracked. Glass lids must not be chipped. Metal lids must not be scratched.

Container: A large container for processing the jars packed with fruit (water bath method) should be large enough to allow the jars to be completely covered with water. Container must have a false bottom (wooden or wire rack) so the bottles do not come in direct contact with the bottom of the container.

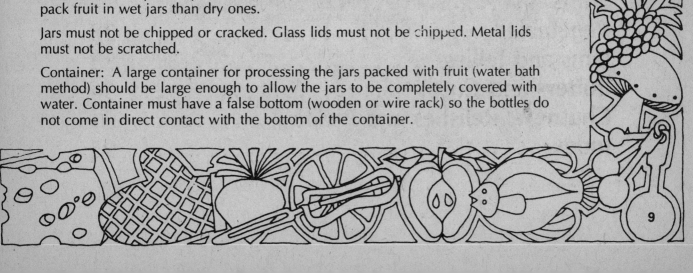

9

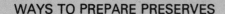

Thermometer: A sugar thermometer is the most useful kind to have if you are planning to bottle fruit and make jams. In the case of bottling fruit, it is necessary to measure the temperature of the water in the water bath method. It can also be used to determine the setting point of jams.

Jar lifter or long handled tongs make it easier to remove the jars from the water bath.

Preparation of Fruit:

Only firm fresh fruit should be used for preserving. The fruit should be washed in cold water and drained in a colander. Hull raspberries. Trim the top and bottom of blackcurrants. Remove pith and peel from citrus fruits and remove any seeds. Pears and apples should be peeled, cored and sliced or quartered. Apricots, peaches and plums can be bottled whole if small enough, or halved and stoned.

Making the Syrup:

For a medium syrup you will need one cup of sugar to each 2½ cups (625 ml) water. Dissolve the sugar in the water over a low heat, stirring constantly. Bring to the boil and boil rapidly for one minute. Strain through a piece of muslin. The amount of sugar may be lessened to make a lighter syrup. (See index for syrup variations.)

Packing the Jars of Bottles:

Fill the jars with the fruit, pressing down gently with a wooden spoon. Do not press too firmly or you may bruise the fruit. Fill the jars to within one inch (2½ cm) of the top. Pour on the syrup and allow the syrup to seep down through the fruit. Tap the jars to make sure that there are no air bubbles. Put on the rubber bands and clip tops or discs and screw bands. If screw bands are being used, tighten them and then unscrew one-half turn to allow steam to escape during the processing.

Methods of Processing:

Water Bath: Arrange the bottles or jars in the container on the wire or wooden rack. Jars must not touch each other or the side of the container. (A piece of cardboard may be placed between the jars.) Pour cold water over the jars making sure that the water covers the jars by about one inch (2½ cm). Cover the container with its lid and put on the stove over a low heat. The temperature of the water should be raised to 130°F (55°C) in one hour and to the required temperature (see chart) in another half hour. The water is then held at this temperature for the required length of time. Take the jars out of the bath with a jar lifter or long handled tongs. If using screw band jars, tighten the screw bands as you remove the jars from the bath. Leave for 24 hours before testing the seal.

Oven Method: Fill the jars or bottles with the fruit and pour on the syrup. Put on the lids but not the clips or screw bands. Put a piece of cardboard or asbestos on the bottom of a baking tin and pour in one inch (2½ cm) of water. Stand the jars in the tin but do not allow them to touch each other or the sides of the tin. Put in the oven at 300°F (150°C) and maintain that heat for the required time (see chart). As soon as the processing is completed, screw on the screw bands or put on the clips.

Remove the jars from the baking tin and put onto a folded cloth or a wooden board. Tighten the screw bands occasionally while the fruit is cooling. Leave for 24 hours before testing the seal.

Pressure Cooker: Fill the jars or bottles in the same way as in the water bath method. Follow the instructions given by the manufacturer of the pressure cooker for bottling. Water should be boiling before putting the jars or bottles on the rack. Do not allow the bottles to touch each other or the sides of the pressure cooker. Cover the cooker and bring to five pounds pressure over a moderate heat. See the chart for the processing time. After the processing time is up, remove the cooker from the heat and allow the pressure to reduce to zero. Carefully remove the lid and tighten the screw bands. Put the bottles on a folded cloth or wooden board to cool. Tighten the screw bands occasionally.

Testing the Seal:

Leave the bottles or jars for 24 hours. Remove the clips or screw bands and lift the jar by the lid. If a complete vacuum has been formed, the lid will be tight. If the lids are loose, a seal has not been made and the contents should be eaten within two days. Or you may reprocess the fruit. But first determine why the seal was not formed. The clips should be thoroughly cleaned, dried and set aside for future use. The screw bands should be washed, dried and lightly oiled, then screwed back on the jars.

Storing:

Be sure to label clearly each bottle or jar with the contents and the date of bottling. Store in a cool, dry, dark place. Light will spoil the color of the fruit and cause the syrup to cloud.

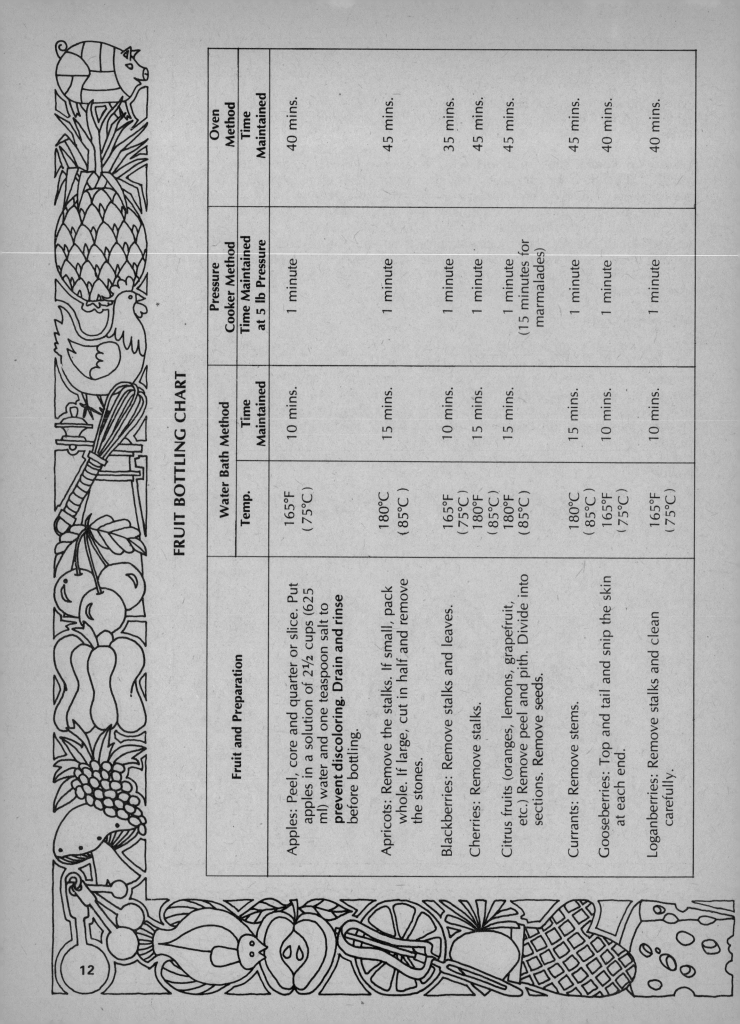

FRUIT BOTTLING CHART

Fruit and Preparation	Water Bath Method		Pressure Cooker Method	Oven Method
	Temp.	Time Maintained	Time Maintained at 5 lb Pressure	Time Maintained
Apples: Peel, core and quarter or slice. Put apples in a solution of 2½ cups (625 ml) water and one teaspoon salt to **prevent discoloring. Drain and rinse** before bottling.	165°F (75°C)	10 mins.	1 minute	40 mins.
Apricots: Remove the stalks. If small, pack whole. If large, cut in half and remove the stones.	180°C (85°C)	15 mins.	1 minute	45 mins.
Blackberries: Remove stalks and leaves.	165°F (75°C)	10 mins.	1 minute	35 mins.
Cherries: Remove stalks.	180°F (85°C)	15 mins.	1 minute	45 mins.
Citrus fruits (oranges, lemons, grapefruit, etc.) Remove peel and pith. Divide into sections. Remove seeds.	180°F (85°C)	15 mins.	1 minute (15 minutes for marmalades)	45 mins.
Currants: Remove stems.	180°C (85°C)	15 mins.	1 minute	45 mins.
Gooseberries: Top and tail and snip the skin at each end.	165°F (75°C)	10 mins.	1 minute	40 mins.
Loganberries: Remove stalks and clean carefully.	165°F (75°C)	10 mins.	1 minute	40 mins.

Fruit and Preparation	Water Bath Method		Pressure Cooker Method	Oven Method
	Temp.	Time Maintained	Time Maintained at 5 lb Pressure	Time Maintained
Peaches: Peel. (Dip into boiling water for ten seconds, then put into cold water for a few seconds. This makes the skin easy to remove.) May be bottled whole, halved or sliced.	180°F (85°C)	15 mins.	3-4 mins.	60 mins.
Pears: Peel, core and quarter or slice. Put into a solution of 2½ cups (625 ml) water and one teaspoon salt to prevent discoloring. Drain and rinse before bottling.	190°F (90°C)	30 mins.	4 mins.	65 mins.
Pineapples: Peel and remove center core. Cut into slices or cubes.	190°F (90°C)	15 mins.	3 mins.	60mins.
Plums: Remove the stalks. Bottle whole or cut in half and remove stones.	165°F (75°C)	15 mins.	1 minute	45 mins.
Raspberries: Remove stalks and carefully clean the berries.	165°F (75°C)	10 mins.	1 minute	40 mins.
Rhubarb: Wipe and cut stalks. (Use young stalks only.)	165°F (75°C)	10 mins.	1 minute	40 mins.
Strawberries: Remove hulls.	165°F (75°C)	10 mins.	1 minute	40·mins.
Tomatoes: Remove stem. Peel, if desired. (Dip the tomatoes into boiling water for ten seconds, then into cold water for a few seconds. This makes them easy to peel.)	190°F (90°C)	30 mins. (if whole) (40 mins. if solid pack)	5 mins. (if whole) (7 mins. if solid pack)	65 mins. (if whole) (75 mins. if solid pack)

Syrup Variations

Basic Syrup

   1 lb (500 g) sugar
   2½ cups (625 ml) water

1. Mix together the sugar and water in a saucepan.
2. Heat, stirring constantly, until the sugar is dissolved.
3. Skim the surface.
4. Boil the mixture to 225°F (110°C). Cool.
5. Store in bottles.

Rum Citrus Syrup

   rind of one orange
   rind of one lemon
   2½ cups (625 ml) basic syrup
   ⅔ cup (165 ml) rum

1. Cut the orange and lemon rinds into strips.
2. Mix together the rinds and basic syrup in a saucepan. Boil for two minutes. Cool.
3. Strain the syrup and stir in the rum.

Blackcurrant Syrup

   1 lb (500 g) blackcurrants
   2½ cups (625 ml) basic syrup

1. Crush the blackcurrants slightly and mix with the basic syrup in a saucepan.
2. Boil for five minutes then allow to cool.
3. When cool, strain.

Cranberry Syrup

1 lb (500 g) cranberries
2½ cups (625 ml) basic syrup
⅓ cup (85 ml) port wine
⅓ cup (85 ml) redcurrant jam

1. Mix together the cranberries and the syrup in a saucepan and boil for five minutes.
2. Remove from heat and stir in the port wine and redcurrant jam.
3. Allow to cool, then strain.

Pineapple Syrup

1 lb (500 g) fresh pineapple
    (cut into cubes)
2½ cups (625 ml) water
1 lb (500 g) sugar

1. Mix together all the ingredients in a saucepan.
2. Bring to a boil (225°F/110°C). Skim the top.
3. Allow to cool, then strain.

Lemon Syrup

5 lemons
2½ cups (625 ml) basic syrup

1. Squeeze the lemons and cut the rinds into strips.
2. Mix the juice and the rinds with the syrup and allow to stand overnight.
3. Put into a saucepan and boil for five minutes.
4. Allow to cool, then strain.

Ginger Syrup

2½ teaspoons chopped fresh
   root ginger
3 tablespoons lemon juice
2½ cups (625 ml) basic syrup

1. Mix together the ginger, lemon juice and syrup in a saucepan.
2. Boil for five minutes.
3. Allow to cool, then strain.

Tomatoes

2 lb (1 kg) firm small
   tomatoes
1 teaspoon sugar
2 teaspoons salt

1. Plunge the tomatoes into boiling water for ten seconds. Dip into cold water for a few seconds, then peel.
2. Pack the tomatoes into sterilized jars.
3. Sprinkle with sugar and salt.
4. Cover the jars with glass lids and clips or disc tops and screw bands (not completely tight).
5. Put the jars into a container and cover with cold water.
6. Put over a low heat and bring to 190°F (90°C) in 1½ hours. Maintain at this temperature for ½ hour.
7. Remove from the water and tighten the screw bands. Continue to tighten them as the jars cool.
8. Test for seal after twenty four hours by removing the clips or screw bands and lifting the jars by the lids.

(If the tomatoes are large, after peeling, cut in halves or quarters. Pack in the same manner as for whole, but process for 40 minutes instead of 30 minutes.)

Apple Rings

4 lb (2 kg) cooking apples
2 lb (1 kg) green peppers
8 cups (2 liters) cider vinegar
½ cups brown sugar
2½ tablespoons juniper
berries

1. Peel and core the apples and cut them into rings.
2. Seed the green peppers and cut them into rings.
3. Put the apples and peppers in alternate layers in warm sterilized jars.
4. Mix together the vinegar, sugar and juniper berries in a saucepan. Bring to a boil.
5. Immediately pour the liquid over the apple and pepper rings. Allow the liquid to overflow.
6. Seal immediately.
7. Keep for six weeks before using.

Spiced Plums

1½ lb (750 g) plums
2 cups (500 ml) white vinegar
3 cups sugar
3-inch (8-cm) stick cinnamon
1½ teaspoons whole allspice
1½ tablespoons mixed spices

1. Wash the plums and remove the stalks.
2. Mix together the vinegar and sugar in a saucepan.
3. Add the spices and boil until syrupy.
4. Put the plums into sterilized jars.
5. When the syrup is cool, pour it over the plums. Set aside overnight.
6. Strain the syrup from the plums into a saucepan. Bring to a boil.
7. When cool, pour back over the plums. Allow to cool, then pour on more syrup to make sure the plums are completely covered.
8. When cold, cover with plastic lined lids and screw caps.
9. Keep for four months before using.

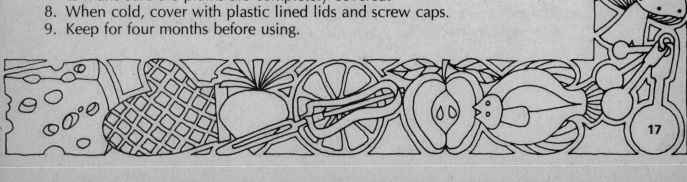

Fruit Salad

¼ lb (125 g) black cherries
¼ lb (125 g) blackberries
¼ lb (125 g) blackcurrants
¼ lb (125 g) redcurrants
¼ lb (125 g) strawberries

¼ lb (125 g) raspberries
4 teaspoons sugar
10 cups (2½ liters) boiled water

1. Thoroughly wash a 2-lb (1-kg) jar, disc lid and screw band. Rinse in boiling water. Do not dry the jar and leave the lid and screw band in the boiled water until ready to use.
2. Cut the cherries in half and remove the stones. Put the cherries in the bottom of the jar and sprinkle with one teaspoon of sugar.
3. Layer the remaining fruit sprinkling on a teaspoon of sugar after each layer (except for the strawberries and raspberries which do not need sugar.)
4. Pour on the boiled water (hot but not boiling) and shake the jar gently to pack fruit and remove any air bubbles.
5. Put on the lid and screw band. Tighten the screw band and then unscrew it half a turn. This allows steam to escape during the processing.
6. Put the jar in a container on a rack and add enough cold water to cover the jar completely.
7. Put onto a low heat and bring to the simmering point. This should take 1½ hours. Hold at the simmering point for five minutes.
8. Remove the jar from the saucepan and tighten the screw band. Tighten every now and then while the jar is cooling. After twenty four hours remove the screw band and test the seal by lifting the jar by the disc lid.

Dried Fruit Compote

½ lb (250 g) dried figs
½ lb (250 g) dried apricots
½ lb (250 g) dried apples
½ lb (250 g) dried peaches

5 cups (1¼ liters) water
1¼ cups clear honey
rind of one lemon

1. Soak the dried fruit in the water overnight. Drain but keep the liquid.
2. Mix together the honey and reserved liquid in a saucepan.
3. Thinly slice the lemon rind and add to the saucepan.
4. Bring the mixture to a boil and boil for five minutes. Remove the rind.
5. Pack the fruit into sterilised jars.
6. Pour the syrup over the fruit to within ½ inch (one cm) of the top. Add a little water if necessary.
7. Put the jars into a large container on a rack. Add enough warm water to come level to the necks of the jars.
8. Slowly bring to a simmer over a low heat. Simmer for five minutes.
9. Put the disc lids and screw bands on the jars not tightening them completely. Simmer for another 25 minutes.
10. Tighten the screw bands and remove the jars from the container. Keep tightening the screw bands as the jars cool.
11. After twenty four hours remove the screw bands and test for a seal by lifting the jars by the disc lid.

Spiced Apples

4 lb (2 kg) sugar
5 cups (1¼ liters) water
⅔ cup (165 ml) ginger wine
1-inch (2½-cm) stick of
  cinnamon
1 blade mace

1 small piece fresh root
  ginger
7 cloves
4 lb (2 kg) cooking apples
rind of two lemons, thinly
  sliced

1. Mix together the sugar, water, ginger wine, cinnamon, mace, ginger and cloves in a saucepan. Boil for ten minutes.
2. Strain the syrup into a large saucepan.
3. Peel and core the apples and cut into eighths.
4. Add the apple sections and lemon rind to the syrup and cook until the apples are tender.
5. Pour into sterilized jars and seal.
6. Keep for one month before using.

Spiced Cherries

2 lb (1 kg) cherries
2½ cups (625 ml) white
  vinegar
1 lb (500 g) raw sugar

1. Remove stalks from cherries.
2. Mix together the vinegar and sugar in a saucepan. Gently heat until the sugar is dissolved.
3. Add the cherries and simmer for about five minutes.
4. Put the cherries into sterilized jars.
5. Boil the liquid until slightly thick and syrupy. Cool.
6. Pour the syrup over the cherries and set aside overnight.
7. Strain the syrup back into a saucepan and bring to the boil. Cool.
8. Pour the syrup back over the cherries. Allow to cool.
9. Add more syrup to make sure that the syrup completely covers the cherries.
10. Cover with plastic lids or glass covers. Metal should never come in contact with the fruit or syrup.
11. Store for two months before using.

Pickled Plums

2 lb (1 kg) plums
rind of ½ lemon
1¼ tablespoons allspice berries
1 small piece fresh root ginger

2½ teaspoons whole cloves
3-inch (8-cm) stick cinnamon
2 teaspoons coriander seeds
2½ cups (625 ml) vinegar
1½ cups brown sugar

1. Wash the plums and remove the stalks.
2. Put the plums into a large enamel saucepan with the lemon rind, spices (tied in muslin) and the vinegar.
3. Slowly bring to the simmering point. Do not boil.
4. Put the plums into sterilized jars.
5. Add the sugar to the liquid and boil until syrupy, stirring frequently. Remove the muslin bag.
6. Pour the syrup over the plums making sure that the plums are completely covered with the syrup.
7. Seal immediately but do not allow metal to come in contact with the plums or the syrup.
8. Keep for about 2½ months before using.

Spiced Orange Slices

5 oranges, thin-skinned	20 cloves
water	5 blades mace
pinch baking soda	4-inch (10-cm) stick cinnamon
1½ cups (300 ml) white vinegar	5 bay leaves
	2 cups sugar

1. Put the oranges into a large saucepan with enough water to cover.
2. Sprinkle on the soda and bring to the boil. Reduce heat and simmer for 45 minutes. Drain but reserve the water.
3. When the oranges are cool, cut them into ¼-inch (½-cm) slices. Cut the slices into halves.
4. Put vinegar, spices (tied in muslin), sugar and 1¼ cups (300 ml) orange liquid into a saucepan and bring to boil. Reduce heat, simmer for 20 minutes.
5. Remove pits from the orange slices. Put the orange slices in the saucepan with the syrup and simmer for ½ hour.
6. Transfer the orange slices and syrup to a bowl and set aside overnight.
7. Remove the bag of spices and put the orange slices into sterilised jars.
8. Boil the liquid again and when cool, pour over the oranges.
9. When cold, cover with two layers of wax paper and one layer of aluminum foil. Tie securely with string. Keep two weeks before using.

Spiced Grapes

2 lb (1 kg) seedless grapes	3-inch (8-cm) stick cinnamon
1¼ cups (300 ml) white vinegar	10 cloves
2 cups sugar	1½ teaspoons grated nutmeg

1. Wash the grapes and remove the stalks.
2. Mix together the vinegar and sugar in a saucepan. Gently heat until the sugar is dissolved, then bring to a boil.
3. Add the grapes and the spices and simmer for five minutes.
4. Put the grapes into sterilized jars and pour the liquid over them. Leave overnight.
5. Strain the liquid from the grapes into a saucepan and bring to a boil. Cool.
6. Remove the cinnamon stick from the grapes.
7. When the liquid is cool, pour back over the grapes.
8. Cover with two layers of wax paper and one layer of aluminum foil. Tie securely with string. Keep for several weeks before using.

Spiced Peaches

2 lb (1 kg) firm peaches
1¼ cups (300 ml) white wine
  vinegar
2 cups sugar
20 whole cloves

7-inch (18-cm) stick
  cinnamon
1 tablespoon whole allspice
extra cloves
extra cinnamon stick

1. Put the peaches in boiling water for a few seconds to facilitate peeling. Remove the skin gently. If the peaches are large, cut in half and remove the seed.
2. Mix together the vinegar, sugar and spices in a large saucepan. Bring to a boil, stirring frequently.
3. Add the peaches and simmer until they are tender.
4. Put the peaches into warm sterilized jars.
5. Boil the spiced liquid until syrupy.
6. Strain into the jars.
7. Put a couple of cloves and a piece of cinnamon stick in each jar.
8. Cover and seal immediately.
9. Keep for about a week before using.

Pears in Syrup

3 lb (1½ kg) sugar
2½ cups (625 ml) water
1 cup (250 ml) lemon juice
rind of three lemons
1-inch (2½-cm) piece root
  ginger
4 lb (2 kg) firm ripe pears

1. Mix together the sugar, water, lemon juice, lemon rind and ginger in an enamel saucepan. Bring to a boil.
2. Peel the pears but leave on the stalks. As each pear is peeled, put into the boiling liquid. (Pears discolor quickly after peeling.)
3. Cover the saucepan and simmer until the pears are tender.
4. Remove the pears from the saucepan and put into warm sterilised jars. (Keep the sauce simmering while you are removing the pears.)
5. Strain the syrup and pour into the jars, making sure that the pears are well-covered with the syrup.
6. Seal immediately.
7. Keep for a few days before using.

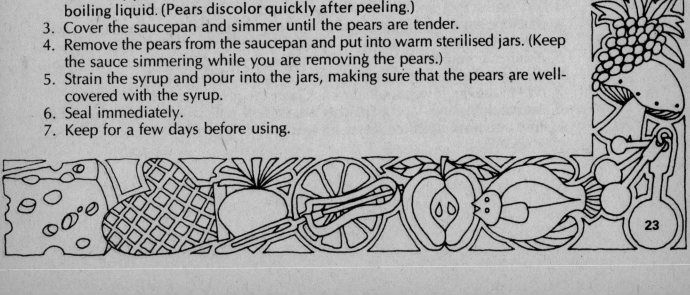

Pears in Almond Syrup

5 cups (1¼ liters) water
½ cup (125 ml) lemon juice
3½ lb (1¾ kg) sugar
¾ lb (375 g) blanched
   almonds
4 lb (2 kg) pears

1. Mix together the water, lemon juice, sugar and half the almonds in a large saucepan.
2. Cook over a low heat, stirring constantly, until the sugar is dissolved.
3. Bring to a boil and boil rapidly until the syrup thickens.
4. Peel, core and cut the pears into eighths.
5. Add to the saucepan with the remaining almonds.
6. Bring to a boil, then reduce the heat and simmer for two minutes.
7. Pour into warm sterilized jars and seal immediately.

Fruit Sauce

3½ lb (1¾ kg) green
   tomatoes, sliced
3 lb (1½ kg) cooking apples,
   peeled, cored and sliced
1 lb (500 g) onions, chopped
½ lb (250 g) dates, chopped
4 cups (1 liter) white vinegar
2 teaspoons coarse salt
1 teaspoon mixed spice

1 tablespoon mustard seeds
1½ teaspoons cloves
¼ teaspoon cayenne
1½ teaspoons ground ginger
1 red chilli
1 blade mace
1½ lb (750 g) brown sugar
2 cups raisins, chopped
2 cups chopped dried currants

1. Mix together the tomatoes, apples, onions, dates, vinegar, salt, mixed spice, mustard seeds, cloves, cayenne, ginger, chilli and mace in a large saucepan.
2. Bring to a boil, stirring constantly. Reduce heat and simmer until very soft.
3. Press the mixture through a sieve and return to the saucepan.
4. Add the sugar, raisins and currants and simmer for about one hour, stirring occasionally.
5. Pour into warm sterilized jars and seal.

Fruity Tomato Sauce

15 medium ripe tomatoes
3 pears, peeled and cored
3 peaches, peeled and pitted
4 medium brown onions,
   peeled

1 red pepper, seeded
1 tablespoon salt
2 cups (500 ml) cider vinegar
2 cups sugar
1 oz (30 g) whole allspice

1. Cut out the stem ends of the tomatoes and peel. Cut the fruits and vegetables into small pieces and put all in a large saucepan.
2. Add the salt, vinegar, sugar and allspice tied in a muslin bag.
3. Bring to a boil. Reduce heat and cook, uncovered, over a medium heat for about 1½ hours or until thick. Stir occasionally.
4. Remove the muslin bag and spoon the sauce into warm sterilized jars. Cover with two layers of wax paper and one layer of aluminum foil. Tie securely with string.
5. May be used in a couple of days.

Mincemeat

2 lb (1 kg) raisins
1 lb (500 g) dried currants
3 oz (90 g) chopped citron
2 lb (1 kg) cooking apples, peeled, cored and finely chopped
1 lb (500 g) minced beef suet
1 lb (500 g) brown sugar
grated rind and juice of two lemons

grated rind and juice of one orange
1 tablespoons allspice
2 oz (60 g) blanched chopped almonds
²/₃ cup (165 ml) dry sherry
½ cup (125 ml) brandy

1. Put all the ingredients except the brandy into a large mixing bowl. Mix very well, cover and set aside for three days. Each day stir the mixture several times.
2. Spoon the mixture into sterilized jars and pour a little brandy into each jar.
3. Seal and leave for about one month before using.

Pear Mincemeat

1½ lb (750 g) pears
1 lb (500 g) dried currants
2 lb (1 kg) raisins
½ lb (250 g) glace apricots, chopped
¼ lb (125 g) glace cherries, chopped
¾ lb (375 g) mixed citron

¾ lb (375 g) shredded suet
1 lb (500 g) brown sugar
2 tablespoons allspice
3 tablespoons cinnamon
1½ tablespoons ground ginger
1½ tablespoons ground cloves
¼ cup (65 ml) brandy
½ cup (125 ml) sherry

1. Peel, core and chop the pears and mix with the remaining ingredients in a large bowl. Allow to stand for 24 hours.
2. Spoon into sterilized jars and seal.
3. Keep for a few weeks before using.

Oranges and Pears Grand Marnier

    4 **lb (2 kg) sugar**
    5 **cups (1¼ liters) water**
  10 **cloves**
    4 **lb (2 kg) firm ripe pears**
    8 **oranges, thick skinned**
    ½ **cup (125 ml) Grand**
        Marnier

1. Mix together the sugar, water and cloves in a saucepan. Boil for ten minutes.
2. Peel and core the pears and cut into quarters.
3. Slice the oranges thinly and remove seeds.
4. Add the pears and the oranges to the syrup and cook until the pears are clear and the syrup is thick.
5. Remove from heat and set aside for three hours.
6. Add the Grand Marnier and return to the boiling point.
7. Put the pears into sterilized jars.
8. Strain the syrup over the pears making sure the pears are completely covered with the syrup.
9. Seal immediately.
10. Keep for a few days before using.

Spiced Tomatoes

  2 **cups sugar**
  ½ **cup (125 ml) water**
  2-inch (5-cm) stick cinnamon
  3-inch (8-cm) piece lemon
    peel
  4 **lb (2 kg) firm tomatoes**

1. Mix together the sugar and water in a large saucepan. Heat, stirring constantly, until the sugar is dissolved.
2. Add the cinnamon stick and lemon peel and bring to a boil.
3. Peel the tomatoes (dip into boiling water for a few seconds) and add to the syrup.
4. Gently cook for twenty minutes. Remove the cinnamon stick and lemon peel.
5. Cook for another 25 minutes, stirring frequently.
6. Remove from heat and allow to cool.
7. Spoon into sterilized jars and seal.

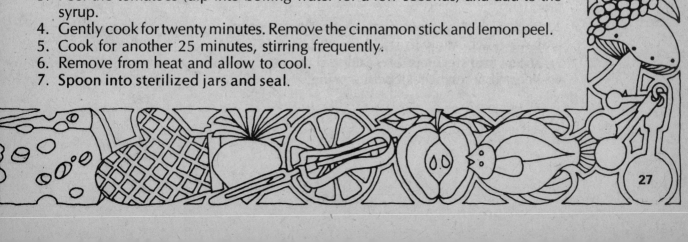

<u>Vegetables</u>

General Hints

Vegetables may only be bottled using a steam pressure canner. This is because the bacteria which causes botulism can only be killed by sterilizing at a temperature of 118°C (240°F). This temperature cannot be reached by the water bath or oven method used in the processing of fruit. Fruit and tomatoes can be bottled at lower temperatures because they contain a natural acid which does not allow the growth of the bacteria responsible for botulism.

All vegetables must be processed at 10 pounds pressure. An adjustment should be made for high altitudes. For every 2,000 feet above sea level, add another one pound of pressure. (e.g. if you live at 2,000 feet above sea level, process at 11 pounds pressure. If you live at 4,000 feet above sea level, process at 12 pounds pressure.)

Read and follow carefully the instructions given by the manufacturer of the steam pressure canner. The following indicate the steps to be taken in the bottling of vegetables, but you must follow the manufacturer's instructions in regard to heating, venting and operating the canner.

Basic Steps for Bottling Vegetables

1. Prepare all the equipment. Discard any jars that are chipped or cracked or lids that are scratched. Sterilize the jars, lids and screw bands. Leave the lids in the boiled water while preparing the vegetables.

2. Put the rack in the bottom of the pressure canner and fill with 2 to 3 inches (5 to 8 cm) of water. Cover canner and bring the water to a boil. Keep hot while preparing the vegetables.

3. Use only the very freshest of vegetables. Do not use any vegetables that are bruised. Thoroughly wash the vegetables several times in cold water.

4. Prepare the vegetables according to the chart and pack into sterilized jars leaving about ½-inch (1-cm) of head space.

5. Pour on the boiling cooking liquid (the liquid in which the vegetables were cooked) or boiling water. Run a wooden handle down the sides of each jar to release any air bubbles. Add more liquid if necessary.

6. Wipe the rims and threads of the jars to make sure any food particles are removed.

7. Put on lids and screw bands according to the manufacturer's instructions.

8. Place the jars on the rack in the pressure canner ensuring that they do not touch each other or the sides of the canner.

9. Follow the manufacturer's instructions for covering and venting the canner and bringing the pressure to ten pounds.

10. When the canner has reached the required pressure, process for the time indicated on the chart. Do not allow the pressure to fall below that required for processing.

11. When the processing time is up, remove the canner from the heat to another range element (never to a cold surface). Allow the pressure to reduce slowly to zero. Open petcock or remove weighted gauge and allow the pressure canner to sit for 15 minutes. Carefully open the canner tilting the lid away from you so the steam goes out the other side.

12. Remove the jars from the canner with a jar lifter or long handled tongs. Put them on a folded cloth or wooden board. When jars are cool, remove the screw bands.

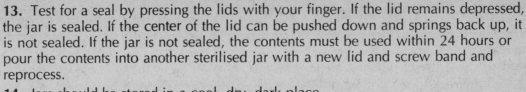

13. Test for a seal by pressing the lids with your finger. If the lid remains depressed, the jar is sealed. If the center of the lid can be pushed down and springs back up, it is not sealed. If the jar is not sealed, the contents must be used within 24 hours or pour the contents into another sterilised jar with a new lid and screw band and reprocess.

14. Jars should be stored in a cool, dry, dark place.

15. All bottled vegetables should be boiled for 15 minutes before eating.

Equipment for Bottling Vegetables

1. Steam Pressure Canner

2. Bottling jars, lids (lacquered metal discs with rubber band attached) and screw bands to secure the discs.

3. Large saucepan for precooking the vegetables.

4. Jar lifter or long handled tongs for removing the jars from the canner.

Signs of bottled food spoilage:

1. Bulging or corroded lid

2. Oozing food

3. Food that looks moldy or mushy

4. Bubbles in the bottle (sign of gas pressure)

5. Unpleasant odor

6. Change in color.

If any of these signs are present, throw away the food immediately. DO NOT TASTE.

VEGETABLE BOTTLING CHART

Vegetable	How to Prepare	Processing at 10 lbs pressure	
		2 cups	4 cups
Artichoke hearts	Remove outer leaves to the heart. Precook for five minutes in boiling water with vinegar (¾ cup vinegar to 4 quarts water). Drain. Pack into hot sterilized jars. Cover with boiling brine made by adding ¾ cup vinegar or lemon juice and 2 tablespoons salt to 4 quarts water. Fill to within ½ inch (1-cm) of top. Seal.	25	25
Asparagus	Trim and cut tough ends. Wash very well in several changes of cold water. Cut into 1-inch (2½-cm) lengths or cut whole spears ¾ inch (2 cm) shorter than jar. Precook for 1 – 3 minutes in boiling water, then put into cold water. Pack into warm sterilized jars. Add salt (½ teaspoon for ½-quart jars; 1 teaspoon for 1-quart jars) and fill with boiling water to within ½ inch (1 cm) of top of jars. Seal.	28	32
Beans, green	Wash the beans very well. Trim off ends and either leave whole or cut into 1-inch (2½-cm) pieces. Precook beans in boiling water for five minutes. Drain and pack into hot sterilized jars. Add salt (½ teaspoon for ½-quart jars; 1 teaspoon for 1 quart jars) and cover beans with boiling water leaving ½ inch (1-cm) of head space. Seal. (You may pack the beans raw but they must be cut into 1 inch (2½-cm) lengths. Add salt and boiling water as in the hot pack.)	25	30
Beets	Cut off tops leaving roots and 1 inch (2½ cm) of stem. Wash very well. Put into a large saucepan with boiling water and cook for 15—25 minutes or until tender. Dip into cold water and remove the skins. Trim the ends and roots. Slice or cube. Pack in hot sterilized jars to within ½ inch (1 cm) of top. Add salt (½ teaspoon to ½-quart jars; 1 teaspoon to 1-quart jars) and pour on boiling water. Seal.	35	40
Carrots	Wash very well, peel or scrape and slice or dice. Hot pack: In a large saucepan cover carrots with boiling water. Bring back to a boil, then pack in hot sterilized jars. Add salt (½ teaspoon for ½-quart jars; 1 teaspoon for 1-quart jars) and cover with the boiling cooking liquid or boiling water to within ½ inch (1 cm) of top. Cold pack: Pack carrots to within ½ inch (1 cm) of top of jars. Add salt (½ teaspoon for ½-quart jars; 1 teaspoon for 1-quart jars) and cover with boiling water. Seal.	30	30
Celery	Wash well and cut off leafy tops and coarse string. Slice or cut into lengths ¾ inch (2 cm) shorter than the jars.	35	35

Vegetable	How to Prepare	Processing at 10 lbs pressure	
		2 cups	4 cups
	Hot pack: blanch the slices for 1—3 minutes. Drain and pack into hot sterilized jars. Add salt (½ teaspoon for ½-quart jars and 1 teaspoon for 1-quart jars.) Add cooking liquid or boiling water and seal. Cold pack: Pack slices or lengths in hot sterilized jars and add salt and water as for hot pack. Seal.		
Corn	Remove husks and silk. Cut raw kernels from the cobs. Put kernels into a saucepan and cover with brine (1 tablespoon salt to 1 quart water). Bring to a boil and pack into hot sterilized jars covering the corn with the brine. Seal.	55	70
Mushrooms	Trim stems and soak in cold water to cover for ten minutes. If small, leave whole; if large, halve or quarter. Steam for four minutes or gently cook in a covered saucepan without water for 15 minutes. Pack into hot sterilized jars and add salt (½ teaspoon for a ½-quart jar). Do not use litre jars. Pour on boiling cooking liquid or boiling water. Seal.	30	
Onions, small white	Peel and cook in boiling water with vinegar (¾ cup vinegar to 4 quarts water) for five minutes. Drain and reserve cooking liquid. Pack into hot sterilized jars. Add four tablespoons salt to each four quarts of cooking liquid and pour over onions. Seal.	25	25
Peas	Shell and wash thoroughly. Hot pack: Cook in a little boiling water for 1—4 minutes. Pack into hot sterilized jars and add salt (½ teaspoon for ½-quart jars; 1 teaspoon for 1-quart jars). Pour on boiling cooking liquid or boiling water. Seal. Cold pack: Pack peas to within 1 inch (2½ cm) of top. Add salt as for hot pack and pour on boiling water. Seal.	40	45
Potatoes, new	Peel and cut in half if large. If small, leave whole. Pack raw into hot sterilized jars. Pour on boiling brine (1 tablespoon salt to one quart water) and seal.	35	40
Pumpkin	Peel and remove seeds. Cut flesh into cubes and boil in a little water until tender. Pack cubes into hot sterilized jars and add salt (½ teaspoon for ½-quart jars; one teaspoon for 1-quart jars). Pour on boiling cooking liquid or boiling water. Seal.	55	90
Zucchini	Wash well and trim off the ends. Do not peel. Cut into ½-inch (1-cm) slices. Hot pack: Place in saucepan with just enough water to cover. Bring to a boil. Pack into hot sterilized jars. Add salt (½ teaspoon for ½-quart jars; 1 teaspoon for 1-quart jars). Cover with boiling cooking liquid or boiling water and seal.	30	40
	Cold Pack: Pack slices into hot sterilized jars. Add salt as for hot pack and fill with boiling water. Seal.	25	30

Jams and Jellies

General Hints

Equipment:

1. A large saucepan. The saucepan should be made from aluminum, stainless steel or unchipped enamel. It must be large enough so the fruit plus the sugar only reach half-way up the sides. When the jam boils, it expands. If the saucepan is not big enough, it will overflow.

2. Jars. Any type of jar is suitable. They must be clean, dry and unchipped.

3. Covers. The jars should be covered first with a waxed disc. The screw top may then be put on or you may simply cover with a piece of plastic secured with an elastic band.

4. Jelly bag and large bowl. A jelly bag is necessary in the making of jelly. If a commercial bag is not available, it is possible to make one by tying a large piece of muslin onto the legs of an inverted stool and placing the bowl under it. If a small quantity of jelly is being made, a colander lined with a piece of muslin and placed over a bowl is adequate.

5. Thermometer. A sugar thermometer marked to at least 110°C (225°F) is necessary to test the setting point of jams.

Choosing the fruit to use:

The fruit used in the making of jams and jellies should be fresh, firm and under-ripe rather than over-ripe. Over-ripe fruit is low in pectin, the substance which makes jams and jellies set.

Fruits which have a high pectin content are the easiest to make into jams and jellies. Fruits high in pectin are citrus fruits, cooking apples, cranberries, gooseberries, plums and quinces. Fruits that have a medium pectin content are apricots, blackberries, loganberries and raspberries. Fruits low in pectin are cherries, grapes, figs, pears, pineapples, rhubarb and strawberries. To get a jam with a good set it is advisable to mix fruits that have a low pectin content with those that have a high pectin content. It is also possible to add a commercially produced pectin to fruits low in pectin content. Fruits low in pectin will need extra acid to reach a good set. Acid in fruit helps to extract the pectin.

To measure the pectin content of fruit, simmer a little of the fruit until it is soft and the juice runs out. Take a teaspoon of the liquid and put it into a cup with three teaspoons of methylated spirits. Shake gently and set aside for two minutes. If the liquid clots, the pectin content is high. If it forms into two or three lumps, the pectin content is medium. If it remains liquid, the pectin content is low.

In order to make a well-set jam or jelly from low pectin and low acid fruit, extra pectin can be added in one of four ways:
1. Mix a fruit which is low in pectin with one that has a high pectin content.
2. Add commercially prepared pectin.
3. Add lemon juice or citric acid.
4. Add a stock made from fruits high in pectin content.

Tests for setting:

1. Place a couple of teaspoons of jam on a cold plate. Allow the jam to cool. When it is cold, touch it with your finger. If it wrinkles and skin has formed, it has reached a good set.
2. Dip a wooden spoon into the jam. Wait a few seconds, then tilt the spoon and let the jam drip off. If it forms a heavy clot as it drips from the spoon, the setting point has been reached.
3. Dip a sugar thermometer in hot water first and then into the jam mixture taking care not to touch the bottom of the saucepan. If the jam has reached 108°C (220°F), it is at the setting point.

Basic Steps in Jam Making:

1. Prepare the fruit by removing any stalks or leaves. Stone the fruit. Wipe clean or rinse in cold water. Peel and core where necessary.

2. Cook the fruit with little or no water to soften it and break it down. This extracts the pectin.

3. Add the sugar and cook over a low heat, stirring constantly, until the sugar is dissolved. Do not allow the mixture to boil until the sugar is completely dissolved. Commercially bottled or packaged pectin is added at this point if necessary.

4. Bring the jam to a boil and boil rapidly without stirring until the jam has reached the setting point. This can take from five to twenty minutes.

5. Test for the setting point.

6. Pour the jam into warm jars. Cover and label.

Basic Steps in Jelly Making:

1. Prepare the fruit as for jam.

2. Cook the fruit until very soft — about one hour.

3. Pour the fruit into a jelly bag and allow to drain for several hours or overnight. Never press the fruit through the bag or squeeze the bag. This will cause the jelly to become cloudy.

4. Pour the juice into a large saucepan and add the sugar. The amount of sugar used depends on the pectin content of the juice. If the juice is high in pectin, use 1 lb (500 g) sugar to each 2½ cups (625 ml) juice. For medium pectin content juice, use ¾ lb (375 g) sugar to 2½ cups (625 ml) juice. Low pectin fruit should not be used for making jelly as it will not set well. Heat the juice and sugar over a low heat, stirring constantly, until the sugar dissolves.

5. Bring the jelly to a boil and boil rapidly without stirring for about ten minutes. Test for the set.

6. Remove any scum from the top of the jelly.

7. Pour into warm jars. Cover and label.

Pear and Apricot Jam

　　1　lb (500 g) dried apricots,
　　　　chopped
　　3　lb (1½ kg) pears
　　½　cup (125 ml) lemon juice
　　3½　lb (1¾ kg) sugar

1. Soak the apricots overnight in enough water to cover. Drain, but keep the water.
2. Peel, core and chop the pears. Mix with the apricots and lemon juice and put into a large saucepan.
3. Add a little of the reserved water and cook over a low heat for ten minutes.
4. Add the sugar and cook, stirring constantly, over a low heat until the sugar is dissolved.
5. Bring to a boil and boil rapidly until the setting point is reached.
6. Pour into jars and seal immediately.

Apricot Jam

　　3　lb (1½ kg) apricots
　　1¼　cups (300 ml) water
　　3　lb (1½ kg) sugar

1. Wash the apricots. Cut in half and remove the stones.
2. Crack open three of the stones and remove the kernels. Put the kernels in boiling water for ten seconds. Remove and chop finely.
3. Mix the chopped kernels with the apricots and put into a saucepan with the water. Cook over a low heat until soft.
4. Add the sugar and cook, stirring constantly, over a low heat until dissolved.
5. Bring to a boil and boil rapidly until the setting point is reached (about 15 minutes).
6. Pour into warm sterilized jars and seal immediately.

Apricot and Apple Jam

2 lb (1 kg) fresh apricots
2 lb (1 kg) cooking apples
2½ cups (625 ml) water
4 lb (2 kg) sugar

1. Cut the apricots in half and remove the stones.
2. Peel, core and slice the apples.
3. Mix all the ingredients in a saucepan and cook, stirring constantly, over a low heat until the sugar is dissolved.
4. Bring to a boil and boil rapidly until the jam has reached the setting point (about 35 minutes).
5. Skim the top of the jam and pour into warm sterilized jars. Seal immediately.

Blackberry and Apple Jam

2 lb (1 kg) cooking apples
⅔ cup (165 ml) water
½ cup (125 ml) lemon juice
2 lb (1 kg) blackberries
4 lb (2 kg) sugar

1. Peel, core and slice the apples.
2. Put the apples into a saucepan with the water and lemon juice and simmer for about ten minutes or until tender.
3. Add the blackberries and sugar and cook, stirring constantly, over a low heat until the sugar is dissolved.
4. Bring to a boil and boil rapidly until the setting point is reached.
5. Pour into warm sterilized jars and seal immediately.

Tomato and Apple Jam

3 lb (1½ kg) green tomatoes
3 cups (750 ml) water
2 lb (1 kg) cooking apples
1¼ teaspoons ground ginger
½ teaspoon ground cloves
3½ lb (1¾ kg) sugar

1. Cut the tomatoes into thin slices and put into a saucepan with the water. Cook for five minutes.
2. Peel, core and slice the apples and add to the tomatoes with the ginger and cloves. Cook until soft.
3. Add the sugar and cook over a low heat, stirring constantly, until the sugar is dissolved.
4. Bring to a boil and boil rapidly until the jam reaches the setting point.
5. Pour into warm sterilized jars and seal immediately.

Pineapple, Pear and Lemon Jam

3 lb (1½ kg) pears
1 small pineapple
5 lemons
4 lb (2 kg) sugar
¼ cup (65 ml) kirsch

1. Peel, core and slice the pears. Peel and chop the pineapple.
2. Squeeze the juice from the lemons and grate the rinds.
3. Put the pears, pineapple, lemon juice and rind into a saucepan and simmer for ten minutes.
4. Add the sugar and cook over a low heat, stirring constantly, until the sugar has dissolved.
5. Bring to a boil and boil rapidly until the setting point is reached.
6. Add the kirsch and mix well.
7. Pour into warm sterilized jars and seal immediately.

Apple and Blackcurrant Jam

1½ lb (750 g) cooking apples
1¼ cups (300 ml) water
4 lb (2 kg) blackcurrants
6 lb (3 kg) sugar

1. Peel, core and slice the apples and put into a saucepan with half the water. Cook over a low heat until soft.
2. Remove the stalks from the blackcurrants and wash. Put into a saucepan with the rest of the water and stew until tender.
3. Mix together the blackcurrants and apples.
4. Mix in the sugar and cook, stirring constantly, over a low heat until dissolved.
5. Bring to a boil and boil rapidly until the jam has reached the setting point.
6. Pour into warm sterilized jars and seal immediately.

Plum Jam

3 lb (1½ kg) plums
1½ - 2 cups (375-500 ml) water
3 lb (1½ kg) sugar

1. Wash and stone the fruit and put into a saucepan with the water. (Under-ripe fruit requires more water than ripe juicy fruit.)
2. Cook over a low heat until the plums are soft.
3. Add the sugar and cook, stirring constantly until the sugar is dissolved.
4. Bring to a boil and boil rapidly until the jam reaches setting point.
5. Pour into warm sterilized jars and seal immediately.

Apple and Plum Jam

3 lb (1½ kg) cooking apples
3 lb (1½ kg) plums, stoned
2½ cups (625 ml) water
6 lb (3 kg) sugar
½ cup (125 ml) lemon juice
1¼ teaspoons cinnamon

1. Peel and core the apples and cut into slices.
2. Tie the apple cores in a muslin bag.
3. Put the apple slices, cores and plums into a saucepan. Add the water and cook over a low heat until the fruit is reduced to pulp.
4. Mix in the sugar, lemon juice and cinnamon and stir until sugar dissolves.
5. Boil rapidly until jam reaches setting point.
6. Pour into warm sterilized jars and seal immediately.

Strawberry Jam

4 lb (2 kg) strawberries
2½ cups (625 ml) juice from
    stewed rhubarb
4 lb (2 kg) sugar

1. Hull the strawberries but do not wash them.
2. Mix the strawberries with the juice and simmer for about ten minutes.
3. Add the sugar and cook, stirring constantly, over a low heat until the sugar is dissolved.
4. Bring to a boil and boil rapidly without stirring for about four minutes.
5. Test for a set.
6. If ready, pour into warm sterilized jars and seal immediately.

Apple and Raspberry Jam

2 lb (1 kg) cooking apples
½ cup (125 ml) lemon juice
⅔ cup (165 ml) water
2 lb (1 kg) raspberries
4 lb (2 kg) sugar

1. Peel, core and slice the apples.
2. Simmer the apples with the lemon juice and water until tender.
3. Add in the raspberries and sugar and stir until the sugar is dissolved.
4. Bring to a boil and boil until the setting point is reached.
5. Pour into warm sterilized jars and seal immediately.

Raspberry Jam

3 lb (1½ kg) raspberries
1¼ cups (300 ml) redcurrant
   juice
3 lb (1½ kg) sugar

1. Remove any leaves or stems from the raspberries. Do not wash them.
2. Put the raspberries and the redcurrant juice in a saucepan. Bring slowly to a boil.
3. Add the sugar and cook, stirring constantly, until the sugar dissolves.
4. Bring back to a boil and boil rapidly for five minutes.
5. Test for a set.
6. Put into warm sterilized jars and seal immediately.

Peach Jam

1 cooking apple, chopped (peel, core and all)	3 lb (1½ kg) peaches
rind of two lemons, thinly sliced	1¼ cups (300 ml) water
3 cloves	1¼ teaspoons ground cinnamon
	3 lb (1½ kg) sugar

1. Put the chopped apple, lemon rind and cloves into a double thickness muslin bag.
2. Peel the peaches (plunge into boiling water to facilitate peeling), remove the stones and slice.
3. Put the muslin bag, peaches and water into a large saucepan and simmer until the peaches are just soft.
4. Squeeze the muslin bag over the saucepan, then discard.
5. Add the cinnamon and sugar and stir over a low heat until the sugar is dissolved.
6. Bring to a boil and boil rapidly until the setting point is reached (15-20 minutes).
7. Remove from heat and allow to stand for ten minutes.
8. Pour into warm sterilized jars and seal immediately.

Rhubarb Jam

4 lb (2 kg) rhubarb	3 lb (1½ kg) sugar
1 cup (250 ml) water	½ cup finely chopped crystallised ginger
¼ cup (65 ml) lemon juice	
2-inch (5-cm) piece fresh root ginger	

1. Wash and trim the rhubarb and cut into 1-inch (2½-cm) pieces.
2. Put the rhubarb, water and lemon juice into a saucepan and bring to a boil.
3. Peel and slightly crush the ginger and add to the rhubarb.
4. Reduce heat and simmer until the rhubarb is soft. Remove the ginger.
5. Add the sugar and cook over a low heat, stirring constantly, until the sugar is dissolved.
6. Stir in the crystallised ginger and bring to a boil. Boil rapidly for about ten minutes or until the jam has reached the setting point.
7. Pour into warm sterilized jars and seal immediately.

Ginger Pear Jam

3½ lb (1¾ kg) pears
1-inch (2½-cm) piece fresh
   root ginger
rind of two lemons
2½ cups (625 ml) water
½ cup (125 ml) lemon juice
2½ lb (1¼ kg) sugar

1. Peel, quarter and core the pears. Reserve peel and cores.
2. Slightly crush the ginger and cut the lemon rind into thin strips.
3. Put the pear peel and cores, ginger and lemon rind into a muslin bag.
4. Put the pears, muslin bag and water into a large saucepan and bring to a boil. Reduce heat and simmer for ½ hour or until the pears are soft.
5. Squeeze the bag over the saucepan and discard.
6. Add the sugar and cook over a low heat, stirring constantly, until the sugar dissolves.
7. Stir in the lemon juice and bring to a boil. Boil rapidly for about 20 minutes or until the jam has reached the setting point.
8. Remove the scum from the top of the jam and remove the saucepan from the heat. Allow to stand for five minutes. Pour into warm sterilized jars and seal immediately.

Loganberry Jam

6 lb (3 kg) loganberries
6 lb (3 kg) sugar

1. Wash and hull the loganberries.
2. Put into a large saucepan and cook over a low heat, stirring constantly, until the fruit is soft.
3. Add the sugar and stir until the sugar is dissolved.
4. Bring to a boil and boil rapidly about 15 minutes or until the jam has reached the setting point.
5. Skim the surface and pour into warm sterilized jars.
6. Cover and seal immediately.

Fig Preserve

   2 lb (1 kg) fresh green figs
      hot water
   2 lb (1 kg) sugar
   1½ teaspoons grated lemon
      rind
   ¼ cup (65 ml) lemon juice

1. Remove the stalks from the figs and put into a large bowl.
2. Pour on enough hot water to cover completely and allow to soak for five minutes. Drain well and chop.
3. Mix the figs in a large saucepan with the sugar, lemon rind and lemon juice. Cook over a low heat, stirring frequently, for about 1½ hours or until the syrup is thick and clear. (More water may be added if the mixture is too thick.)
4. Remove from the heat and cool completely.
5. When   pour into sterilized jars and seal.

Dried Apricot Jam

   1 lb (500 g) dried apricots
   8 cups (2 liters) water
   ¼ cup (65 ml) lemon juice
   3 lb (1½ kg) sugar
   2 oz (60 g) slivered almonds

1. Chop the apricots and put into a bowl with the water. (Make sure the apricots are completely covered with the water.) Allow to soak for 24 hours.
2. Put the apricots and the water into a large saucepan and simmer for ½ hour or until the apricots are very soft.
3. Add the lemon juice and sugar and cook over a low heat, stirring constantly, until the sugar is dissolved.
4. Stir in the almonds and bring to the boil. Boil rapidly for about 15 minutes or until the jam has reached the setting point.
5. Pour into jars and seal immediately.

Loganberry and Rhubarb Jam

2 lb (1 kg) loganberries
3 lb (1½ kg) rhubarb
1¼ cups (300 ml) water
5 lb (2½ kg) sugar

1. Rinse the loganberries under running water and shake dry. Put into a saucepan and cook over a low heat for five minutes, pressing with a wooden spoon.
2. Wash and dry the rhubarb and cut into chunks. Mix with the water and cook until very soft.
3. Mix together the two fruits in a large saucepan and add the sugar. Cook over a low heat, stirring constantly, until the sugar has dissolved.
4. Bring to a boil and boil rapidly until the jam reaches the setting point.
5. Pour into warm sterilized jars and seal immediately.

Cherry Jam

5 lb (2½ kg) stoned cherries
  (reserve stones)
¾ cup (185 ml) lemon juice
3 lb (1½ kg) sugar

1. Tie the cherry stones in a muslin bag and put into a large saucepan with the cherries and lemon juice.
2. Bring to the boil. Reduce heat and simmer until the cherries are tender (about ½ hour).
3. Remove the bag of cherry stones.
4. Add the sugar to the cherries and cook over a low heat, stirring constantly, until the sugar is dissolved.
5. Bring to a boil and boil rapidly until the jam reaches the setting point.
6. Remove the scum from the top of the jam.
7. Allow the jam to cool completely in the saucepan, then pour into sterilized jars and seal.

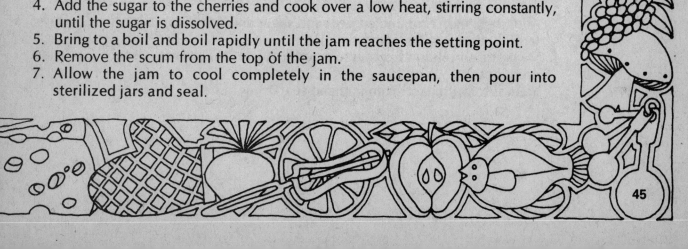

Pumpkin and Apricot Jam

1 lb (500 g) dried apricots
2 lb (1 kg) pumpkin
4 lb (2 kg) sugar
¾ teaspoon ground ginger

1. Soak the apricots in just enough water to cover for 24 hours.
2. Remove the seeds, peel and chop the pumpkin into small pieces. Sprinkle the pumpkin with 1½ lb (750 g) sugar and set aside for 24 hours.
3. Mix together the apricots and their water with the pumpkin, the remaining sugar and the ginger.
4. Heat gently, stirring constantly, until the sugar melts.
5. Simmer until the pumpkin is tender.
6. Bring to a boil and boil rapidly until the jam reaches the setting point.
7. Pour into warm sterilized jars and seal when cold.

Carrot and Rhubarb Conserve

1 lb (500 g) young carrots
1 lb (500 g) young tender
  rhubarb
1 lemon

water
¼ lb (125 g) glace mixed peel
2 lb (1 kg) sugar

1. Wash and dry the carrots and cut into small pieces.
2. Wash and dry the rhubarb and cut into chunks.
3. Grate the lemon rind and chop the flesh finely. Discard the pits and pith.
4. Simmer the carrots, rhubarb, and lemon in just enough water to cover until the carrots are tender.
5. Add the lemon rind, mixed peel and sugar and cook over a low heat, stirring constantly, until the sugar dissolves.
6. Bring to a boil and boil rapidly until the setting point is reached, stirring frequently.
7. Pour into warm sterilized jars and seal immediately.

Special Blackberry Jam

6 cups blackberries
½ cup (125 ml) water
3 lb (1½ kg) sugar
¾ cup (185 ml) orange juice
⅓ cup (85 ml) lemon juice
2 tablespoons grated orange rind

1. Cook the blackberries with the water until heated through.
2. Rub through a strainer and return to the saucepan.
3. Add the sugar and cook over a low heat, stirring constantly, until the sugar is dissolved.
4. Add the orange juice, lemon juice and orange rind. Mix well.
5. Bring to a boil and boil rapidly until the jam has reached the setting point.
6. Pour into warm sterilized jars and seal immediately.

Passionfruit and Pear Jam

4 lb (2 kg) firm pears
24 passionfruit
3½ lb (1¾ kg) sugar

1. Peel, core and dice the pears.
2. Scoop out the passionfruit pulp.
3. Mix together the pears and passionfruit in a large saucepan. Cook over a low heat until soft.
4. Add the sugar and cook, stirring constantly, over a low heat until the sugar dissolves.
5. Bring to a boil and boil rapidly until the jam reaches the setting point.
6. Pour into warm sterilized jars and seal immediately.

Rummy Jam

½ lb (250 g) dried apricots
½ lb (250 g) dried apples
½ lb (250 g) dried peaches
¼ lb (125 g) figs
¼ lb (125 g) glace cherries

10 cups (2½ liters) water
4 lb (2 kg) sugar
¾ cup (185 ml) lemon juice
½ cup (125 ml) rum

1. Chop all the fruit into small pieces.
2. Put into a large bowl and pour on the water. Set aside for 24 hours.
3. Transfer fruit and liquid to a large saucepan and heat until warm.
4. Add the sugar and cook, stirring constantly, over a low heat until the sugar is dissolved.
5. **Bring to a boil and boil rapidly for 20 minutes.**
6. Add the lemon juice and mix well. Continue to boil until the jam has reached the setting point.
7. **Stir in the rum and pour into warm sterilized jars. Seal immediately.**

Pear and Raisin Preserve

2 lb (1 kg) sugar
3 cups (750 ml) water
6 tablespoons honey
2 lb (1 kg) pears

10 whole cloves
3½ tablespoons raisins
1 medium lemon, thinly
  sliced

1. Mix together the sugar and water in a large saucepan. Place over a low heat and cook, stirring constantly, until the sugar has dissolved.
2. **Add the honey and bring to a boil. Boil rapidly for eight minutes.**
3. Peel, core and halve the pears.
4. Put the pears, cloves, raisins and lemon slices into the saucepan with the honey syrup and cook over a medium heat until the pears are tender and the syrup is thick.
5. **Spoon the pears into warm sterilized jars and pour the syrup over them. Seal immediately.**
6. Process by the water bath method.

English Marmalade

7 oranges
2 lemons
15½ cups (3¾ liters) water
6 lb (3 kg) sugar

1. Wash the oranges and the lemons well.
2. Cut off the rind removing as little pith as possible with it. Cut the rind into small chunks. Put into a large saucepan.
3. Remove the pith from the outside of the fruit and put into a large bowl.
4. Cut the orange and lemon pulp into chunks, separating the flesh from the pith and seeds.
5. Put the pulp into the large saucepan with the rind and put the pith and seeds into the large bowl with the pith from the outside of the fruit.
6. Put 12½ cups of the water into the saucepan with the fruit pulp and the remaining water into the bowl with the pith and seeds.
7. Cover and allow to stand for 24 hours.
8. Strain the water from the bowl into the saucepan.
9. Put the pith and seeds into a muslin bag and put into the saucepan.
10. Bring to the boil and simmer for one hour, stirring frequently. Skim the surface.
11. Add the sugar and cook over a low heat, stirring constantly, until the sugar is dissolved.
12. When the sugar is dissolved, simmer for ½ hour, stirring frequently.
13. Remove the muslin bag, squeeze over the saucepan, then discard.
14. Bring to a boil and boil rapidly until the mixture is reduced by half. Remove scum from the surface.
15. Test to make sure the marmalade has reached the setting point, then remove from the heat.
16. When the marmalade begins to form a skin on the top, mix well and pour into warm sterilized jars. Seal when cold.

Rhubarb Marmalade

2 lb (1 kg) tender rhubarb
grated rind of two lemons
4 cups sugar
½ cup (125 ml) lemon juice

1. Trim, wash and dry the rhubarb.
2. Mix the rhubarb, lemon rind and sugar in a large bowl and allow to stand overnight.
3. Transfer to a large saucepan and stir in a lemon juice.
4. Cook over a low heat, stirring constantly, until the sugar is dissolved.
5. Bring to a boil and boil rapidly until the marmalade has reached the setting point.
6. Pour into warm sterilized jars and seal immediately.

Lemon Marmalade

1½ lb (750 g) lemons
8 cups (2 liters) water
3 lb (1½ kg) sugar

1. Wash the lemons and cut off the rind taking care to remove as little pith with the rind as possible. Cut the rind into thin strips.
2. Remove the pith and cut into small pieces.
3. Cut the pulp into slices and remove seeds and inner pith.
4. Tie all the pith and seeds in a muslin bag.
5. Put the pulp, the peel and the muslin bag into a large bowl and pour on the water. Allow to stand overnight.
6. Put into a saucepan and boil for about 1¼ hours or until the peel is tender.
7. Remove the bag and squeeze over the saucepan.
8. Add the sugar and cook over a low heat, stirring constantly, until the sugar is dissolved.
9. Bring to a boil and boil rapidly until the setting point is reached.
10. Remove the saucepan from the heat and allow to stand until a skin forms on the top.
11. Stir well, then pour into warm sterilized jars. Seal immediately.

Three-Fruit Marmalade

1 grapefruit
2 lemons
1 sweet orange
8 cups (2 liters) water
3 lb (1½ kg) sugar

1. Wash and peel the fruit. Cut the rinds into thin strips. Chop the pulp. Put the pith, cores and seeds into a muslin bag.
2. Soak the pulp, rind and muslin bag in the water overnight.
3. Put into a saucepan and simmer for 1½ to 2 hours or until the rind is soft.
4. Add the sugar and cook, stirring constantly, over a low heat until the sugar is dissolved.
5. Bring to a boil and boil rapidly until the marmalade reaches the setting point. Remove from heat.
6. Allow the marmalade to sit for five minutes. Stir with a sterilized spoon and pour into warm sterilized jars. Seal immediately.

Lemon-Carrot Marmalade

3 large lemons quartered and seeded
2 lb (1 kg) carrots, peeled
3 cups sugar
½ cup (125 ml) honey
¼ cup minced, preserved ginger
8 cups (2 liters) water

1. Mince together the lemons and carrots or grind together in a meat grinder using the coarsest blade.
2. Combine all the ingredients in a large saucepan and cook over a low heat, stirring constantly, until the sugar is dissolved.
3. Bring to a boil and boil rapidly until the marmalade reaches the setting point.
4. Remove from heat and allow to sit for five minutes.
5. Give the marmalade a stir, then pour into warm sterilized jars. Seal immediately.

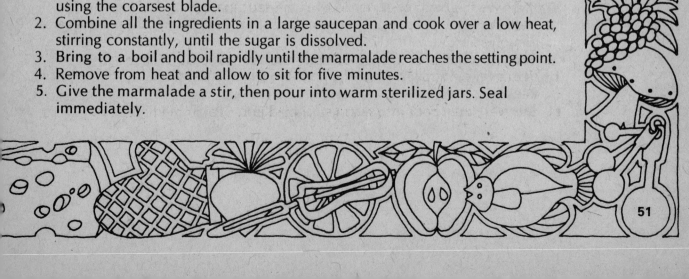

Mint Jelly

4 lb (2 kg) rhubarb
5 cups (1¼ liters) water
½ cup (125 ml) lemon juice
8 tablespoons finely chopped
    mint
sugar
green food coloring

1. Chop the rhubarb and mix with the water and lemon juice in a large saucepan.
2. Bring to a boil. Reduce heat and simmer for ½ hour.
3. Stir in the mint and simmer for another three minutes.
4. Pour into a jelly bag and allow to drain for at least 12 hours.
5. Measure the juice and pour into a clean large saucepan.
6. For every 2½ cups (625 ml) juice you will need 1 lb (500 g) of sugar.
7. Add the sugar and heat, stirring constantly, until the sugar is dissolved.
8. Bring to a boil and boil rapidly until the jelly reaches the setting point.
9. Remove from the heat and add a few drops of coloring.
10. Pour into warm sterilized jars and seal immediately.

Mandarin Jelly

3 lb (1½ kg) mandarins
1 lemon
½ oz (15 g) citric acid
11 cups (2¾ liters) water
3½ lb (1¾ kg) sugar

1. Chop up the mandarins and the lemon into small bits, peel, pith and all.
2. Mix together the mandarins, lemon, citric acid and water in a large bowl and allow to soak overnight.
3. Transfer to a large saucepan and simmer for about 1½ hours or until the lemon rind is tender.
4. Pour the mixture into a jelly bag and allow to drip for at least 12 hours.
5. Pour the juice into a large saucepan and add the sugar.
6. Heat gently, stirring constantly, until the sugar is dissolved.
7. Bring to a boil and boil rapidly until the jelly has reached the setting point.
8. Pour into warm sterilized jars and seal when cold.

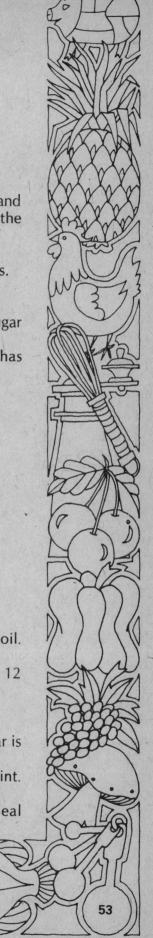

Rosemary Jelly

5 lb (2½ kg) cooking apples, sliced
2½ cups (625 ml) water
6 tablespoons fresh rosemary leaves
1 cup (250 ml) malt vinegar
sugar
5 drops green food coloring

1. Put the apples, water and half the rosemary leaves into a large saucepan and bring to a boil. Reduce heat and simmer for about 45 minutes or until the fruit is pulpy.
2. Add the vinegar and boil for five minutes.
3. Pour the mixture into a jelly bag and leave to drip for at least 12 hours.
4. Measure the juice and pour into a clean saucepan.
5. For every 2½ cups (625 ml) juice add 1 lb (500 g) sugar.
6. Add the sugar to the juice and heat gently, stirring constantly, until the sugar has dissolved.
7. Bring to a boil and boil rapidly for about ten minutes or until the jelly has reached the setting point.
8. Skim the top.
9. Stir in the remaining rosemary leaves and green coloring.
10. Pour into warm sterilized jars and seal immediately.

Apple Jelly

3 lb (1½ kg) cooking apples
3 cups (750 ml) water
3 tablespoons lemon juice
sugar

1. Wash the apples and cut into chunks. (Do not peel or core.)
2. Put the apples into a large saucepan with the water and bring to a boil. Reduce heat and simmer until the apples are tender (about 20 minutes).
3. Pour the apples and liquid into a jelly bag and allow to drip for at least 12 hours.
4. Measure the juice and pour into a clean saucepan.
5. For every 2½ cups (625 ml) of juice add 1 lb (500 g) sugar.
6. Stir in the lemon juice and sugar. Heat, stirring constantly, until the sugar is dissolved.
7. Bring to a boil and boil rapidly until the jelly reaches the setting point. Remove from the heat.
8. Skim the foam off the top and pour into warm sterilized jars. Seal immediately.

Mulberry Jelly

1 lb (500 g) mulberries
1 cooking apple, chopped
½ cup (125 ml) water
sugar

1. Mix together the mulberries, apple and water in a large saucepan. Simmer, covered, for about 20 minutes or until the mulberries are soft.
2. Pour the mixture into a jelly bag and leave to drip for at least 12 hours.
3. Measure the juice and pour into a clean saucepan.
4. For every 2½ cups (625 ml) juice, add 1 lb (500 g) sugar.
5. Add the sugar to the juice and cook, stirring constantly, over a low heat until the sugar is dissolved.
6. Bring to a boil and boil rapidly until the jelly has reached the setting point (about ten minutes).
7. Remove the scum from the top of the jelly.
8. Pour into warm sterilized jars and seal immediately.

Redcurrant Jelly

4 lb (2 kg) redcurrants
2½ cups (625 ml) water
sugar

1. Wash the redcurrants and put into a large saucepan with the water.
2. Simmer until the fruit is very soft (about one hour).
3. Mash the redcurrants and pour into a jelly bag. Allow to drain for at least 12 hours.
4. Measure the juice and pour into a clean saucepan. Heat the juice.
5. For every 2½ cups (625 ml) juice add 1 lb (500 g) sugar.
6. Add the sugar to the juice and cook, stirring constantly, over a low heat until the sugar is dissolved.
7. Bring to a boil and boil rapidly for about ten minutes or until the jelly has reached the setting point.
8. Pour into warm sterilized jars and seal immediately.

Grape Jelly

3 lb (1½ kg) green grapes,
  crushed
1¼ cups (300 ml) white wine
1½ lb (750 g) cooking apples

1 lemon
5 cardamom seeds
sugar
¾ cup (185 ml) brandy

1. Mix together the grapes and white wine in a large saucepan. Simmer for ½ hour or until the grapes are pulpy.
2. Slice the apples, lemons and cardamoms and simmer for 20 minutes or until the apples are very soft.
3. Pour into a jelly bag and allow the juice to drip into a bowl for at least 12 hours.
4. Measure the juice and pour into a clean saucepan.
5. For every 2½ cups (625 ml) of juice add 1 lb (500 g) sugar. Stir over a low heat until the sugar is dissolved, stirring constantly.
6. Bring to a boil and boil rapidly for about ten minutes or until the jam has reached the setting point.
7. Pour into warm sterilized jars and seal immediately.

Blackberry and Apple Jelly

3 lb (1½ kg) blackberries
750 g (1½ lb) cooking apples
water
sugar

1. Wash the blackberries and drain them well.
2. Wash the apples and chop them coarsely. Do not peel or core.
3. Mix the blackberries with the apples in a large saucepan.
4. Pour on just enough water to cover the fruit.
5. Bring to a boil. Reduce heat and simmer until the fruit is tender (about 25 minutes).
6. Mash the fruit well in the saucepan.
7. Pour into a jelly bag and allow to drip for at least 12 hours.
8. Measure the juice and pour into a clean saucepan.
9. For each 2½ cups (625 ml) juice you will need 1 lb (500 g) sugar.
10. Add the sugar and cook over a low heat, stirring constantly, until the sugar is dissolved.
11. Bring to a boil and boil rapidly until the setting point is reached. Skim the top of the jelly.
12. Pour into warm sterilized jars and seal when cold.

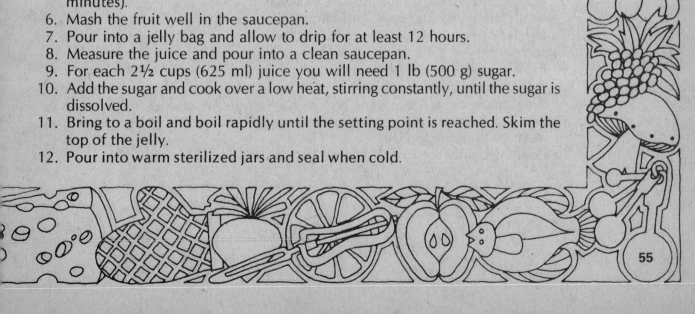

Butters and Curds

Pear Butter

16 pears
2 cups (500 ml) water
3 lb (1½ kg) sugar
1 teaspoon ground cloves

2 teaspoons ground cinnamon
¾ teaspoon ground ginger
3 tablespoons lemon juice

1. Wash the pears well and cut into quarters. Do not peel or core them.
2. Put into a large saucepan and add the water. Cover and cook over a medium heat for about ½ hour or until tender.
3. Press the pears through a colander and measure the pulp. Return the pulp to a saucepan.
4. Put 1½ cups of the sugar in a separate saucepan and cook until it melts and caramelizes. Pour into the pears.
5. Add the cloves, cinnamon, ginger and remaining sugar. Mix well and cook, uncovered, until thick, stirring frequently.
6. Remove from the heat and stir in the lemon juice.
7. Pour into warm sterilized jars and seal.

Apple and Sage Butter

4 lb (2 kg) cooking apples	⅔ cup (165 ml) water
1 cup sugar	¼ cup (65 g) butter
2 teaspoons salt	¾ teaspoon Worcestershire
1½ teaspoons pepper	sauce
2½ teaspoons dried sage	4 tablespoons vinegar
1 medium onion, chopped	

1. Peel, core and chop the apples.
2. Mix the apples with the rest of the ingredients in a large saucepan.
3. Cook over a low heat until the apples are very soft.
4. Beat until smooth and creamy, then bring to the boil.
5. Pour into warm sterilized jars and seal immediately.

Cinnamon Apple Butter

4 lb (2 kg) cooking apples
¼ cup (65 g) butter
1 cup sugar
3½ teaspoons cinnamon
5 whole cloves
1¼ cups (300 ml) water

1. Peel, core and chop the apples.
2. Put into a large saucepan with the rest of the ingredients and cook over a low heat until the apples are very soft.
3. Remove the cloves.
4. Beat the mixture until smooth and creamy.
5. Bring to a boil, then pour into warm sterilized jars and seal immediately.

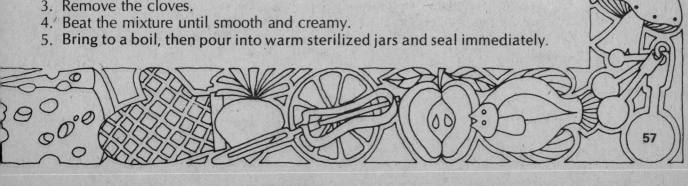

Apricot Butter

2 oz (60 g) dried apricots	¼ cup (65 g) butter
pinch of baking soda	2 eggs, beaten
boiling water	2 tablespoons lemon juice
1 cup sugar	grated rind of half lemon

1. Chop the apricots and put into a bowl with the pinch of baking soda and just enough boiling water to cover. Allow to stand for 1½ hours. Drain but reserve the water.
2. Rinse the apricots in running water and put into a saucepan.
3. Cook in as little reserved soaking water as necessary until tender.
4. Press through a strainer.
5. Add the sugar, butter, eggs, lemon juice and grated rind.
6. Put into the top of a double boiler and cook over simmering water, stirring constantly, until thick.
7. Pour into warm sterilized jars and seal immediately.

Lemon Curd

6 large lemons
1½ cups (375 g) butter, cut
   into small cubes
2 lb (1 kg) sugar
8 eggs, beaten

1. Squeeze the juice from the lemons and cut the rinds into thin strips.
2. Put the lemon juice, lemon rinds, butter, sugar and eggs into the top of a double boiler.
3. Put over very hot (not boiling) water and cook, stirring constantly, until the butter has melted and the sugar has dissolved.
4. Pour the mixture through a strainer and discard the rinds.
5. Return to a clean double boiler top and cook over very hot water, stirring frequently, until the mixture is thick and smooth.
6. Pour into warm sterilized jars and seal immediately. (Use within four months.)

Raspberry and Apple Curd

3 lb (1½ kg) cooking apples
¾ cup (185 ml) lemon juice
grated rind of three lemons
1½ lb (750 g) raspberries

1¼ cups (300 g) butter
5 eggs, beaten
1¾ lb (875 g) sugar
1 cup (250 ml) water

1. Peel, core and chop the apples.
2. Mix the apples with the lemon juice and grated rind in a saucepan. Bring to a boil. Reduce heat and simmer until the apples are tender.
3. Beat the apple mixture until smooth.
4. Put the raspberries into a saucepan and gently heat until soft. (If thawed frozen raspberries are used, this is not necessary.)
5. Press the raspberries through a strainer. Discard the seeds.
6. Mix together the apple mixture and the raspberries in the top of a double boiler.
7. Add the butter, eggs, sugar and water. Place over simmering water and cook, stirring constantly, until thick.
8. Pour into warm sterilized jars and seal immediately.

Orange Curd

6 oranges	1½ cups (375 g) butter, cut
1½ tablespoons lemon juice	into small cubes
2½ teaspoons orange-flower	2 lb (1 kg) sugar
water	9 eggs, beaten

1. Squeeze the juice from the oranges and cut the rind into thin strips.
2. Mix together the orange rinds, orange juice, lemon juice, orange-flower water, butter and sugar in the top of a double boiler.
3. Place over very hot (not boiling) water and stir until the butter has melted and the sugar dissolved.
4. Beat in the eggs a little at a time.
5. Pour the mixture through a strainer. Discard the rinds.
6. Return to the double boiler and cook over a low heat, stirring frequently (constantly towards the end), until the curd is thick.
7. Pour into warm sterilized jars and seal immediately.

Cranberry Cheese

6 lb (3 kg) cranberries	1½ tablespoons lemon juice
water	1¼ teaspoons ground
6 lb (3 kg) sugar	cinnamon
½ cup (125 ml) orange juice	½ teaspoon ground mace
grated rind of one orange	

1. Trim and wash the cranberries.
2. Put into a large saucepan with enough cold water to cover them. Crush with the back of a spoon.
3. Bring to a boil. Reduce heat and simmer until the berries are very soft. Crush occasionally during the cooking.
4. Press the mixture through a strainer and return the puree to a clean saucepan. (If the puree is thin, thicken it by boiling rapidly.)
5. Stir in the sugar and cook over a low heat, stirring constantly, until the sugar is dissolved.
6. Add the orange juice, orange rind, lemon juice, cinnamon and mace.
7. Bring to a boil. Then reduce the heat and simmer until the cranberry cheese is stiff.
8. Pour into small jars and seal.

Chutneys, Relishes and Pickles

General Hints

Equipment:

Enamel or aluminum saucepan should be used. Brass, copper, tin or iron are not suitable.

Wooden spoons should be used for stirring and mixing.

Ordinary glass jars are suitable for storing. They should be thoroughly washed in hot soapy water, rinsed well and then sterilised.

Ordinary screw tops can be used but metal should never come in contact with the contents. A waxed disc should be put between the contents and the lid. A convenient covering for chutneys, relishes and pickles is two layers of wax paper and one layer of aluminum foil tied with string.

General Information:

Uncooked pickles should be kept for about one month before using. Cooked chutneys, relishes and pickles can be eaten immediately but improve in flavor if kept for a couple of days.

Coarse salt is always better to use. Refined table salts contain additives which can affect the flavor.

Never make pickles with unboiled vinegar.

Vegetables will absorb a little vinegar so be sure to cover the vegetables generously with vinegar. There should be about ½ inch (one cm) covering the top of the solid.

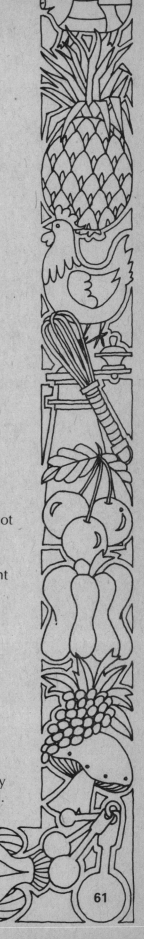

Tomato and Apple Chutney

3 lb (1½ kg) tomatoes
3 lb (1½ kg) cooking apples, cored
1 lb (500 g) onions
1 medium green pepper
1½ cups raisins

1 cup raw sugar
1¼ tablespoons coarse salt
1½ teaspoons grated fresh root ginger
2 teaspoons pickling spice
5 cups (1¼ liters) vinegar

1. Chop together the tomatoes, apples, onions, pepper and raisins.
2. Put into a saucepan with the sugar, salt and spices (tied in a piece of muslin). Mix well.
3. Add the vinegar, stir well and bring to a boil.
4. Simmer, uncovered, until the mixture is reduced to a thick consistency (about 1¼ hours).
5. Remove the muslin bag of spices and press the mixture through a strainer.
6. Pour into sterilized jars and seal.

Pear Chutney

3 lb (1½ kg) pears
1¼ cups (300 ml) wine vinegar
¾ cup (185 ml) lemon juice
1¼ cups brown sugar
1 cup sultana raisins
1 cup chopped dates
½ lb (250 g) walnut halves
2 teaspoons salt

1. Peel, core and dice the pears.
2. Mix the pears together with the rest of the ingredients in a large saucepan.
3. Bring to a boil. Reduce the heat and simmer for about one hour or until the mixture is thick.
4. Pour into warm sterilized jars and cover immediately with two layers of wax paper and one layer of aluminum foil. Tie securely with string.

Spiced Apple Chutney

1 lb (500 g) onions, minced
5 lb (2½ kg) apples, peeled
   and chopped
1½ cups (375 ml) water
1¼ teaspoons ground ginger
2 teaspoons coarse salt

1¼ tablespoons dry mustard
10 cloves
8 whole allspice
2 cups (500 ml) vinegar
2½ cups brown sugar

1. Mix together the onions, apples, water, ginger, salt and mustard in a large saucepan.
2. Put the cloves and allspice into a muslin bag and add to the saucepan.
3. Bring to a boil. Reduce heat and simmer for 45 minutes.
4. Stir in the vinegar and sugar and simmer uncovered, for 1½ hours.
5. Remove the muslin bag and, when cool, pour the chutney into sterilized jars and seal.
6. May be eaten in a few days.

Mint Apple Chutney

2 lb (1 kg) apples
2½ cups mint leaves
½ lb (250 g) onions
½ lb (250 g) tomatoes
1 lb (500 g) dried currants

2½ cups (625 ml) vinegar
2½ teaspoons dry mustard
2 teaspoons coarse salt
2 cups brown sugar

1. Peel the apples and remove the cores.
2. Chop the apples finely with the mint leaves, onions, tomatoes and currants. Put into a saucepan.
3. Add 1¾ cups of the vinegar, mustard and salt and cook until soft.
4. Heat the remaining vinegar and pour over the sugar. Stir until dissolved.
5. Add the sugar mixture to the saucepan and continue cooking until thick.
6. Pour into sterilized jars when cool. Cover with two layers of wax paper, then one layer of aluminum foil. Tie securely with string.
7. May be eaten immediately.

Red Pepper and Apple Chutney

4 lb (2 kg) apples	1½ tablespoons black treacle
1 lb (500 g) red peppers	2½ cups (625 ml) vinegar
1½ lb (750 g) onions	1¼ tablespoons coarse salt
1½ cups raisins	pinch cayenne
⅔ cup sultana raisins	cinnamon stick
⅔ cup dried currants	mustard seeds
2½ cups brown sugar	

1. Peel and core the apples and chop finely.
2. Seed and chop the peppers with the onions, raisins and sultana raisins.
3. Put the apples, peppers, onions, raisins, sultana and currants into a saucepan with the sugar, treacle, vinegar, salt and pinch of cayenne.
4. Simmer for one hour, stirring frequently.
5. Pour into jars and put a few of the remaining spices into each jar.
6. Cover the jars with two layers of wax paper and one layer of aluminum foil. Tie securely with string.
7. May be eaten immediately.

Summer Squash Chutney

1 lb (500 g) summer squash	1 tablespoon salt
2 cooking apples	pinch cayenne
2 medium tomatoes, peeled	½ teaspoon ground cloves
3 medium onions	1½ cups mixed dried fruit
2 cups sugar	2½ cups (625 ml) malt vinegar

1. Peel and core the squash and apples.
2. Chop the squash and apples with the tomatoes and onions.
3. Put this mixture into a saucepan with the remaining ingredients.
4. Cook over a low heat, stirring constantly, until the sugar is dissolved.
5. Bring to a boil. Reduce heat and simmer for two hours, stirring occasionally.
6. Pour into warm sterilized jars and cover with two layers of wax paper and one layer of aluminum foil when cool. Tie securely with string.

Special Green Tomato Chutney

3 lb (1½ kg) green tomatoes
½ lb (250 g) onions
2 tablespoons salt
2 lb (1 kg) cooking apples
1 lb (500 g) brown sugar
½ lb (250 g) sultana raisins

2 oz (60 g) mustard seeds
    (soaked for 3 hours)
4 chillies, chopped
1 teaspoon ground ginger
2½ cups (625 ml) vinegar

1. Coarsely mince the onions and tomatoes and put into a large bowl.
2. Sprinkle with the salt and set aside for 24 hours. Strain.
3. Put the onions, tomatoes and remaining ingredients into a large saucepan and bring to a boil. Reduce heat and simmer for 1½ hours.
4. Pour into warm sterilized jars and when cool, cover with two layers of wax paper and one layer of aluminum foil. Tie securely with string.

Apple Chutney

3 lb (1½ kg) apples, peeled
    and cored
½ lb (250 g) onions
2 cups (500 ml) spiced
    vinegar (see index)
1¼ cups brown sugar

⅔ cup sultana raisins
2 teaspoons coarse salt
1 teaspoon coriander seeds
2 pieces fresh root ginger
2 teaspoons dry mustard

1. Chop together the apples and onions.
2. Put into a saucepan with half the vinegar. Simmer until tender.
3. Add the sugar, sultana raisins, salt, coriander seeds, ginger and mustard and the remaining vinegar. Simmer for about 20 minutes, uncovered.
4. Remove the pieces of ginger and pour into sterilized jars while hot. Cover with two layers of wax paper and screw top metal lid or aluminum foil.
5. May be used in a few days.

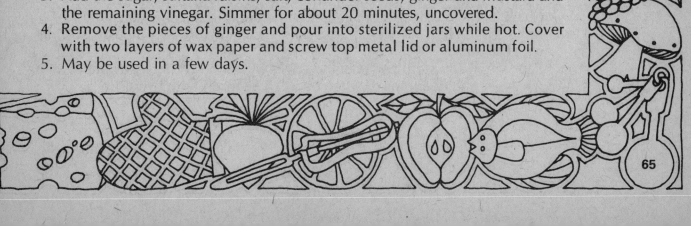

Sweet Chutney

3 lb (1½ kg) green apples	1 tablespoon chopped
1 lb (500 g) raisins	preserved ginger
½ lb (250 g) onions	2 teaspoons dry mustard
1 lb (500 g) tomatoes, skinned	¼ teaspoon cayenne
2½ lb (1¼ kg) brown sugar	1¼ tablespoons coarse salt
¾ cup currants	4 cups (1 liter) vinegar
1¼ teaspoons ground cloves	

1. Peel the apples and remove the cores and seeds. Put into a saucepan with about ½ cup (125 ml) water and cook until tender. Drain.
2. Chop the raisins with the onions and tomatoes. Put into the saucepan with the apples. Mix well.
3. Add the remaining ingredients, cover and simmer gently for about 1½ hours, stirring occasionally.
4. Pour into warm sterilized jars. Cover with two layers of wax paper and one layer of aluminum foil. Tie securely with string.
5. May be used immediately.

Apricot and Orange Chutney

2 lb (1 kg) dried apricots	2½ teaspoons coriander
(chopped and soaked)	seeds, crushed
5 oranges	1 tablespoon coarse salt
3 medium onions, chopped	⅔ cup raisins
3 cups raw sugar	2½ cups (625 ml) vinegar

1. Put the oranges whole into boiling water. Boil for five minutes. Remove from water and cool.
2. Peel the oranges and cut the peel into thin strips.
3. Remove the pith and chop the oranges into small bits. Be sure to collect all the juice. Remove the seeds.
4. Strain the apricots and put them in a saucepan with the oranges and remaining ingredients. Mix well.
5. Bring to a boil. Reduce heat and simmer for about one hour or until the chutney is thick and the apricots are soft. Stir frequently.
6. Pour the chutney into warm sterilised jars. When cool, cover with two layers of wax paper and one layer of aluminum foil. Tie securely with string.
7. Keep for a couple of days before eating.

Chinese Chutney

3 lb (1½ kg) gooseberries
½ lb (250 g) onions
2 cups brown sugar
4 cups (1 liter) spiced vinegar
(see index)

1 tablespoon mustard seeds
1½ tablespoons coarse salt
1 cup raisins

1. Trim and wash the gooseberries.
2. Chop the onions.
3. Put the gooseberries, onions and the remaining ingredients into a saucepan and mix well.
4. Simmer, uncovered, until smooth and thick, stirring frequently.
5. Pour into warm sterilized jars.
6. Cover with two layers of wax paper and one layer of aluminum foil. Tie securely with string.
7. May be eaten in a few days.

Orange Chutney

4 navel oranges
3 apples
2 medium onions, chopped
1⅓ cups brown sugar
⅔ cup raisins

¼ cup ground ginger
½ teaspoon crushed chillies
2½ cups (625 ml) vinegar
1½ tablespoons coarse salt
⅛ teaspoon black pepper

1. Grate the rind of the oranges.
2. Remove the pith, skin and seeds and cut the oranges into small chunks.
3. Peel the apples and remove the cores and seeds. Cut into small pieces.
4. Put the oranges, grated rind, apples and onions into an enamel saucepan with the rest of the ingredients. Mix well.
5. Bring to a boil. Reduce heat and simmer until the mixture is reduced to a pulp, stirring frequently.
6. Pour into warm sterilized jars. When cool, cover with two layers of wax paper and one layer of aluminum foil. Tie securely with string.
7. May be eaten immediately.

Apple and Dried Fruit Chutney

2 lb (1 kg) apples (after peeling and coring)
1 lb (500 g) raisins
½ lb (250 g) dates, chopped
½ lb (250 g) apricots (chopped and soaked)

4 medium onions, chopped
6 cups (1½ liters) vinegar
½ teaspoon crushed chillies
2 pieces fresh root ginger
2½ cups brown sugar

1. Mix together the apples, raisins, dates, apricots, onions and vinegar in a large saucepan.
2. Wrap the chillies and ginger in a piece of muslin. Add to the apple mixture.
3. Bring to a boil. Reduce the heat and simmer until the apples are very soft, stirring frequently. Remove the chillies and ginger.
4. Add the sugar and boil for ten minutes until the chutney is thick, stirring frequently.
5. Pour the chutney into hot sterilized jars.
6. When cool, cover with two layers of wax paper and one layer of aluminum foil. Tie securely with string. May be eaten after a few days.

Lemon Chutney

2 lb (1 kg) lemons
1 lb (500 g) onions
1½ cups raisins
3½ tablespoons coarse salt
5 cups (1¼ liters) spiced vinegar (see index)

1 tablespoon mustard seeds
¾ teaspoon ground ginger
3¼ cups sugar

1. Squeeze the lemons and discard the seeds.
2. Chop the lemon rind, pith and pulp finely with the onions and raisins. Put into a bowl.
3. Sprinkle salt over the lemon mixture and pour on lemon juice. Mix well.
4. Pour on the spiced vinegar to cover mixture. Cover and set aside overnight.
5. Pour the mixture into a saucepan and add the mustard seeds and ginger. Cover and simmer for about one hour or until the lemon pieces are tender.
6. Mix the sugar with the remaining spiced vinegar. Add to the saucepan and boil for about 15 minutes or until the mixture thickens, stirring constantly.
7. Pour into warm sterilized jars and cover with two layers of wax paper and one layer of aluminum foil while still hot. Tie securely with string.
8. Keep for a few days before using.

Bombay Chutney

1 lb (500 g) green apples
1 lb (500 g) onions
1 lb (500 g) dates
1¼ teaspoons cayenne
1½ teaspoons ground ginger

1 teaspoon dry mustard
5 cups (1¼ quarts) spiced
vinegar (see index)
2½ cups brown sugar

1. Peel the apples and remove the cores.
2. Chop the apples with the onions and dates.
3. Mix the cayenne, ginger and mustard with a tablespoon of the spiced vinegar. Set aside.
4. Put the apples, onions and dates in a saucepan with the vinegar. Bring to a boil. Reduce heat and simmer until the mixture is soft.
5. Add the sugar and the cayenne mixture. Boil for three minutes, stirring constantly.
6. Pour into warm sterilized jars. Cover with two layers of wax paper and one layer of aluminum foil. Tie securely with string.
7. May be used after a couple of days.

Rhubarb Chutney

2 lb (1 kg) coarsely chopped
rhubarb
1 cup chopped onions
1 cup raisins
2 cups brown sugar

½ cup (125 ml) cider vinegar
1 teaspoon salt
¾ teaspoon ground cinnamon
½ teaspoon ground ginger
½ teaspoon ground allspice

1. Combine all the ingredients in a large saucepan.
2. Heat gently, stirring constantly, until the sugar is dissolved.
3. Bring to a boil. Reduce heat and simmer over a medium heat for about ½ hour or until the mixture is thick. Stir frequently.
4. Pour into warm sterilized jars and cover with two layers of wax paper and one layer of aluminum foil. Tie securely with string.
5. May be eaten immediately.

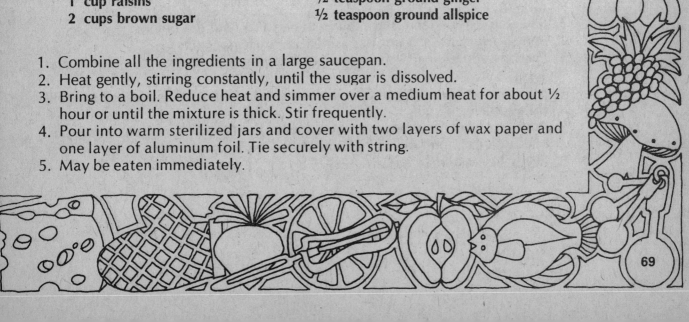

Red Tomato Chutney

3 lb (1½ kg) ripe tomatoes	2¾ cups brown sugar
½ lb (250 g) onions	1½ tablespoons coarse salt
¾ lb (375 g) cooking apples	1 teaspoon dry mustard
1 cup raisins	4 cups (1 liter) spiced vinegar
1 cup sultana raisins	(see index)

1. Peel and chop the tomatoes.
2. Chop the onions and mix with the tomatoes.
3. Peel the apples and remove the cores. Chop coarsely.
4. Mix together the apples, raisins, sultana raisins, sugar, salt, mustard and vinegar in a saucepan and bring to a boil.
5. Add the tomatoes and onions and simmer for one hour or until thick. Stir frequently.
6. Pour into warm sterilized jars and cover with two layers of wax paper and one layer of aluminum foil while still hot. Tie securely with string.
7. Keep for a couple of days before using.

Apple and Marrow Chutney

3 lb (1½ kg) marrow (after peeling and seeding)	2 lb (1 kg) apples (after peeling and coring)
1½ lb (750 g) onions, chopped	1½ lb (750 g) brown sugar
2½ tablespoons coarse salt	6 cups (1½ liters) spiced vinegar (see index)

1. Slice the marrow and put into a shallow dish with the onions.
2. Sprinkle with the salt and set aside for 24 hours. Strain.
3. Slice the apples and put into a large saucepan with the marrow, onions and sugar.
4. Add half the vinegar and cook until the apples are very soft, stirring occasionally.
5. Add the rest of the vinegar and cook until the mixture is thick.
6. Pour into jars and seal while still hot.
7. Ready to eat immediately.

Nectarine and Peach Chutney

1½ lb (750 g) peaches
1½ lb (750 g) nectarines
1 lb (500 g) brown sugar
2 cups (500 ml) white vinegar
4 tablespoons grated fresh
  root ginger
1 clove garlic, minced

2½ teaspoons cinnamon
2 teaspoons ground cloves
1¼ teaspoons salt
¼ teaspoon pepper
2 medium onions, chopped
1 green pepper, chopped

1. Wash the peaches and nectarines. Remove the seeds and chop the fruit.
2. Mix together the sugar, vinegar, ginger, garlic, cinnamon, cloves, salt and pepper in a large saucepan. Slowly bring to the boil, stirring constantly.
3. Stir in the onions, pepper, peaches and nectarines.
4. Return to a boil. Reduce heat and simmer over a medium heat for about one hour or until thick, stirring frequently.
5. Pour into warm sterilized jars and cover with two layers of wax paper and one layer of aluminum foil. Tie securely with string.

Green Tomato Chutney

1 lb (500 g) onions, chopped
5 lb (2½ kg) green tomatoes
2 teaspoons coarse salt
2 cups sugar
5 cups (1¼ liters) spiced
  vinegar (see index)
1 cup raisins

1. Simmer the onions in a little water until soft. Drain.
2. Peel and slice the tomatoes and put into the saucepan with the onions and salt. Mix well.
3. Bring to a boil. Reduce heat and simmer for ten minutes.
4. Mix the sugar with the vinegar. Add to the tomatoes.
5. Stir in the raisins and simmer for about one hour or until thick. Stir frequently.
6. Pour the chutney into warm sterilized jars while still hot. Cover with two layers of wax paper and one layer of aluminum foil. Tie securely with string.
7. May be used immediately.

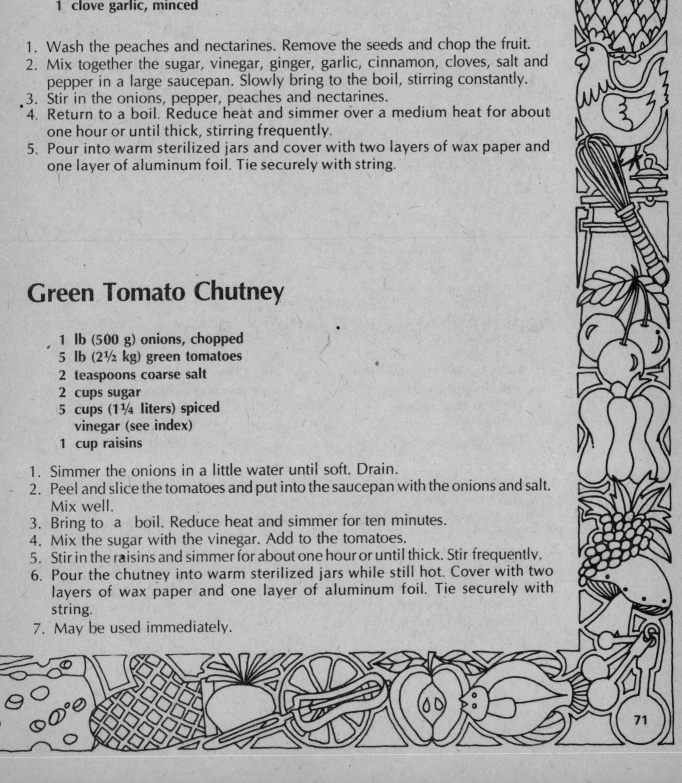

Prune and Apple Chutney

4 lb (2 kg) cooking apples,
peeled, cored and chopped
1 lb (500 g) prunes, pitted and
soaked

2 cups (500 ml) vinegar
1 cup (250 ml) lemon juice
1½ cups sugar
2 teaspoons coarse salt

1. Mix together the apples and prunes in a large saucepan.
2. Add the vinegar, lemon juice, sugar and salt. Stir well.
3. Bring to a boil. Reduce heat and simmer for about one hour or until thick.
4. Pour into warm sterilized jars and seal immediately.
5. Keep for a couple of days before using.

Tomato Chutney

2 cups brown sugar
½ cup (125 ml) cider vinegar
½ cup (125 ml) tarragon
vinegar
3 tablespoons grated fresh
root ginger
2 cloves garlic, minced
2 teaspoons curry powder
½ teaspoon cinnamon
2 tablespoons salt
1 tablespoon pepper

4 lb (2 kg) tomatoes, red and
green
1 lb (500 g) cooking apples
½ lb (250 g) dried figs,
chopped
½ lb (250 g) prunes, chopped
¼ lb (125 g) dried currants
½ cup raisins
⅓ cup (85 ml) lemon juice
grated rind of two lemons

1. Mix together the sugar and vinegars in a saucepan. Cook over a low heat, stirring constantly, until the sugar is dissolved.
2. Add the ginger, garlic, curry powder, cinnamon, salt and pepper and bring to a boil. Boil rapidly for two minutes.
3. Peel and chop the tomatoes. Peel, core and chop the apples.
4. Put the tomatoes and apples into a large saucepan with the figs, prunes, currants, raisins, lemon juice and grated lemon rind.
5. Pour the vinegar mixture over the tomato mixture and bring to a boil. Reduce heat and simmer for about three hours, stirring occasionally.
6. Spoon into warm sterilized jars and cover with two layers of wax paper and one layer of aluminum foil. Tie securely with string.

Apricot Chutney

2½ lb (1¼ kg) apricots, pitted and quartered
500 g (1 lb) brown onions, peeled and diced
2 cups sultana raisins
1 lb (500 g) brown sugar

2 cups (500 ml) cider vinegar
1 teaspoon chilli powder
2 teaspoons mustard seeds
1¼ teaspoons salt
1 teaspoon turmeric
¾ teaspoon cinnamon

1. Mix together all the ingredients in a large saucepan.
2. Bring to a boil. Reduce heat and simmer for about one hour, uncovered, or until juice has thickened.
3. Pour into warm sterilized jars and cover with two layers of wax paper and one layer of aluminum foil. Tie securely with string.
4. May be eaten immediately but flavor improves after a few days.

Cantaloupe Chutney

4 lb (2 kg) cantaloupe rind
1¾ kg (3½ lb) sugar
2 cups dried currants
2 teaspoons powdered allspice
5 cups (1¼ liters) white vinegar

1 teaspoon salt
2 large oranges, coarsely diced
2 large green peppers, seeded and diced

1. Peel and cut enough cantaloupe rind (including ¼ inch/5 mm of the pulp) to make 4 lb.
2. Cut the rind into bite-sized pieces and put into a large saucepan with enough water to cover. Boil for 12 minutes. Drain.
3. Add the remaining ingredients to the cantaloupe, cover and simmer over a medium heat for 45 minutes.
4. Remove the cover and simmer for another 45 minutes or until the juice has thickened.
5. Pour into warm sterilized jars and seal.

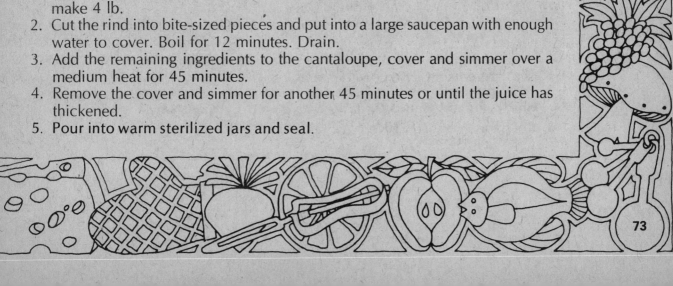

Corn and Cabbage Relish

2 lb (1 kg) corn kernels
1 lb (500 g) cabbage, chopped
½ lb (250 g) celery, chopped
2 large red peppers, seeded
2 large green peppers, seeded

2 medium onions
1½ cups sugar
1½ tablespoons coarse salt
1¼ tablespoons dry mustard
4 cups (1 liter) vinegar

1. Chop all the vegetables.
2. Mix together the vegetables and the remaining ingredients in a large saucepan.
3. Bring to a boil. Reduce heat and simmer until the corn is tender.
4. When cool, pour into jars. When cold, cover with two layers of wax paper and one layer of aluminum foil. Tie securely with string.
5. May be used within a few days.

Plum-Papaya Chutney

1¼ cups (300 ml) cider vinegar
1¾ cups sugar
½ cup sultana raisins
2 cloves garlic, minced
2 tablespoons chopped crystallised ginger

2-inch (5-cm) piece cinnamon stick
1½ teaspoons salt
⅛ teaspoon cayenne
2 lb (1 kg) ripe papayas
2 lb (1 kg) red plums

1. Mix together the vinegar, sugar, sultana raisins, garlic, ginger, cinnamon stick, salt and cayenne in a large saucepan.
2. Bring to a boil. Reduce heat and simmer, uncovered, for about 1½ hours or until thickened. Stir frequently.
3. Peel and seed the papayas and cut into cubes. Quarter the plums and remove the seeds.
4. Add the papayas and plums to the syrup and simmer for about 30 minutes, stirring frequently. Remove cinnamon stick.
5. Pour into warm sterilized jars and cover with two layers of wax paper and one layer of aluminum foil. Tie securely with string.
6. Keep for a few days before using.

Mint Chutney

1 lb (500 g) brown onions, peeled
1 lb (500 g) unripe apples, peeled and cored
½ lb (250 g) green tomatoes, stemmed
2 cups (packed) fresh mint leaves
2 cups raisins
2 teaspoons salt
2 teaspoons prepared mustard
2 cups (500 ml) cider vinegar
2 cups sugar

1. Chop together onions, apples, tomatoes, mint leaves and raisins or grind in a meat grinder using the coarsest blade.
2. Put into a large saucepan with the salt, mustard and vinegar.
3. Simmer over a low heat for about 30 minutes or until the vegetables are tender.
4. Add sugar and stir until the sugar is dissolved.
5. Bring to a boil and boil rapidly until liquid is reduced to half and is slightly syrupy.
6. Pour into warm sterilized jars and seal.

Mango and Peach Chutney

1½ cups sugar
1½ cups (375 ml) white vinegar
2 small onions, chopped
1 green pepper, chopped
1 clove garlic, minced
1 lemon, thinly sliced
1½ teaspoons ground cinnamon
½ teaspoon ground cloves
½ teaspoon ground allspice
1 teaspoon salt
⅛ teaspoon cayenne
½ cup sultana raisins
2½ lb (1¼ kg) ripe mangoes
2 lb (1 kg) peaches

1. In a large saucepan, mix together the sugar, vinegar, onions, pepper, garlic, lemon, cinnamon, cloves, allspice, salt, cayenne and sultana raisins.
2. Cook over a low heat, stirring constantly, until the sugar dissolves.
3. Bring to a boil. Reduce heat and simmer, uncovered for about one hour or until thick, stirring occasionally.
4. Peel and slice the mangoes and peaches removing the seeds and stones.
5. Add mangoes and peaches to the syrup and simmer until the fruit is tender — about ½ hour.
6. Pour into warm sterilized jars and cover with two layers of wax paper and one layer of aluminum foil. Tie securely with string.

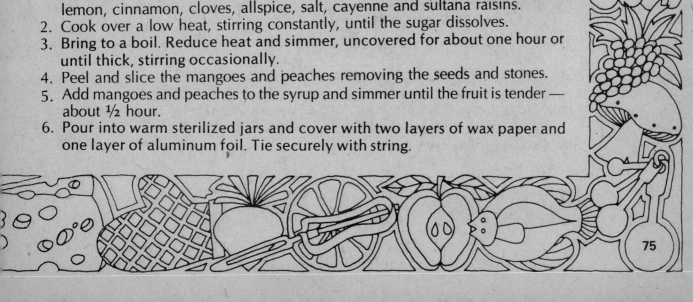

Mixed Vegetable Relish

4 large green tomatoes
2 green peppers, seeded
1 red pepper, seeded
1 lb (500 g) white onions, peeled
2 large carrots, peeled
3 medium cucumbers, peeled and seeded

1 cauliflower, separated in flowerets
8 tablespoons plain flour
8 tablespoons brown sugar
1 teaspoon turmeric
4 tablespoons prepared mustard
3 cups (750 ml) cider vinegar

1. Cut out the stem end of the tomatoes and chop them with the rest of the vegetables.
2. Put into a large bowl and cover with well-salted water. Allow to stand overnight.
3. Transfer the vegetables and the brine into a large saucepan and bring to a boil. Drain.
4. Mix together the flour, sugar, turmeric and mustard in a large saucepan.
5. Slowly add the vinegar, stirring constantly, and cook over a medium heat until thickened.
6. Add the drained vegetables and mix well. Cook over a low heat until the mixture is thick and the vegetables tender.
7. Pour into warm sterilized jars and cover.

Corn Relish

10 large (or 15 small) ears tender young corn
1 medium green pepper, seeded and minced
½ medium red pepper, seeded and minced

2 teaspoons salt
1¼ teaspoons dry mustard
1⅓ cups (335 ml) cider vinegar
1 cup sugar
½ teaspoon turmeric

1. Scrape the corn kernels from the cobs.
2. Mix the corn kernels with the remaining ingredients in a large saucepan and bring to a boil.
3. Reduce heat and simmer for 30 minutes.
4. Pour into warm sterilized jars and cover.

Spiced Tomato Relish

1 lb (500 g) tomatoes
1 medium green pepper
1 lb (500 g) onions
1 lb (500 g) apples
3 cloves garlic
1¼ cups (300 ml) vinegar
1½ cups sugar
1½ tablespoons coarse salt

1 tablespoon paprika
1 teaspoon cayenne
1½ tablespoons prepared
 English mustard
½ teaspoon mixed spice
1 can (6 oz/185 g) tomato
 paste

1. Peel the tomatoes and cut them into chunks.
2. Remove the seeds from the pepper and chop with onions, apples and garlic.
3. Put the tomatoes, pepper, onions, apples and garlic into a saucepan with the vinegar. Simmer for about ½ hour or until thick.
4. Stir in the remaining ingredients and boil for three minutes, stirring constantly.
5. Pour into warm sterilized jars and cover with two layers of wax paper and one layer of aluminum foil while still hot. Tie securely with string.
6. Keep for a couple of days before using.

Orange-Pineapple Chutney

3 large oranges
2 cups (500 ml) vinegar
1 cup brown sugar
2 small onions, chopped
1 clove garlic, minced
1 teaspoon salt
½ teaspoon ground cloves

½ teaspoon ground allspice
⅛ teaspoon cayenne
1 stick cinnamon (2 inches long)
1 cup chopped pitted dates
½ cup sultana raisins
4 lb (2 kg) pineapple

1. Remove the thin outer rind of one orange and cut into thin pieces. Set aside.
2. Remove the peel and pith of all the oranges and separate into sections.
3. Mix together the vinegar, sugar, onions, garlic, salt, ground cloves, allspice, cayenne, cinnamon stick, dates and sultana raisins in a large saucepan.
4. Bring to a boil, stirring constantly.
5. Add the orange rind and simmer for ½ hour or until slightly thickened.
6. Prepare the pineapple and cut into small cubes.
7. Add pineapple to the syrup and simmer, uncovered 1½ hours or until thick.
8 Add the orange sections and simmer for ten minutes.
9. Put into warm sterilized jars and cover with two layers of wax paper and one layer of aluminum foil. Tie securely with string.

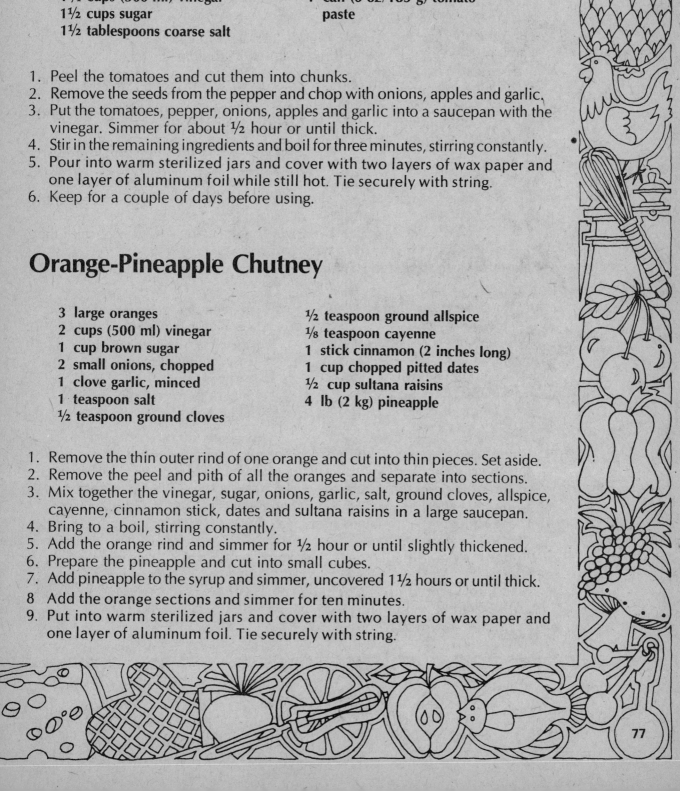

Cucumber Relish

12 large cucumbers, peeled
5 medium onions
5 green peppers, seeded
1 tablespoon celery seeds
1 tablespoon mustard seeds
1 teaspoon salt

½ teaspoon ground cloves
1 tablespoon ground
   turmeric
4 cups (1 liter) cider vinegar
2½ cups sugar

1. Chop together the cucumbers, onions and green peppers.
2. Combine the vegetables and the remaining ingredients in a large saucepan and bring to a boil, stirring constantly.
3. Reduce the heat and simmer for about 2½ hours.
4. Pour into warm sterilized jars and cover with two layers of wax paper and one layer of aluminum foil. Tie securely with string.
5. May be eaten immediately.

Zucchini Relish

5 lb (2½ kg) zucchini
8 medium onions
½ cup salt
cold water
2 cups (500 ml) white wine
   vinegar
1 cup sugar

1 teaspoon dry mustard
2 teaspoons celery seeds
½ teaspoon ground cinnamon
½ teaspoon nutmeg
½ teaspoon pepper
½ lb (250 g) canned pimientos,
   chopped

1. Chop together the zucchini and onions.
2. Mix the zucchini and onions in a large bowl with the salt and cover with cold water. Cover and refrigerate overnight.
3. Drain the vegetables and rinse with cold water. Drain thoroughly.
4. Put the zucchini and onions in a large saucepan with the remaining ingredients. Mix well.
5. Bring to a boil. Reduce heat and simmer, uncovered, for about ½ hour, stirring frequently.
6. Pour into warm sterilized jars and cover with two layers of wax paper and one layer of aluminum foil. Tie securely with string.
7. Keep for a few days before using.

Pepper Relish

12 medium green peppers,
   seeded
12 medium red peppers,
   seeded
12 small brown onions,
   peeled

2¼ cups (565 ml) cider
   vinegar
2⅔ cups sugar
2 tablespoons salt

1. Mince together the peppers and onions.
2. Put the peppers and onions into a large bowl and pour on enough boiling water to cover. Set aside for five minutes.
3. Mix together the vinegar, sugar and salt in a large saucepan.
4. Heat gently, stirring constantly, until the sugar is dissolved. Bring to a boil.
5. Drain the peppers and onions and add to the vinegar mixture.
6. Return to a boil and boil rapidly for five minutes.
7. Pour finto warm sterilized jars and cover.

Cantaloupe and Pear Relish

2 lb (1 kg) cantaloupe rind
2½ lb (1¼ kg) under-ripe
   pears
4 lb (2 kg) sugar

2 tablespoons dry mustard
8 cups (2 liters) water
2 cloves garlic

1. Cut up enough cantaloupe rind (including 5 mm/¼ inch of the pulp) to make 2 lb. Cut into 1-inch (2½-cm) squares, cover with cold salted water (¼ cup salt to 4 cups water) and allow to stand overnight.
2. Drain the rind and put into a large saucepan.
3. Peel and core the pears and cut into ½-inch (1-cm) cubes. Put into the saucepan with the cantaloupe rind.
4. Cover with fresh water and cook over a medium heat for 30 minutes. Drain.
5. Mix together the sugar, mustard and water in a large saucepan and heat, stirring constantly, until the sugar is dissolved.
6. Add the drained fruit and garlic cloves and bring to a boil. Reduce heat and simmer for 2½ hours or until the cantaloupe is translucent and the juice syrupy.
7. Remove the garlic and pour into warm sterilized jars. Cover with two layers of wax paper and one layer of aluminum foil. Tie securely with string.
8. May be eaten immediately.

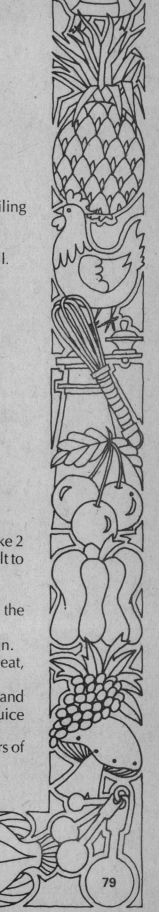

Tomato Relish

4 lb (2 kg) tomatoes
2 medium onions, chopped
3 medium cooking apples, peeled, cored and sliced
1½ lemons, thinly sliced
2½ tablespoons grated fresh root ginger
2 cloves garlic, minced

¼ cup sugar
2 teaspoons salt
1 tablespoon mustard seeds
½ teaspoon ground cloves
¼ teaspoon cayenne
¾ cup (185 ml) white vinegar
¾ cup (185 ml) honey

1. Peel the tomatoes by blanching for 15 seconds in boiling water and them dipping in cold water. Cut out the stems.
2. Mix together the tomatoes, onions, apples, lemons, ginger, garlic, sugar, salt, mustard seeds, cloves, cayenne, vinegar and honey in a large saucepan.
3. Bring to a boil. Reduce heat and simmer, uncovered, over a low heat for about five hours. Stir frequently.
4. Pour into warm sterilized jars and cover with two layers of wax paper and one layer of aluminum foil. Tie securely.
5. May be eaten immediately.

Frankfurter Relish

4 cups minced onions
4 cups minced cabbage
4 cups finely chopped green tomatoes
8 medium green peppers, chopped
6 medium red peppers, chopped

½ cup salt
3 lb (1½ kg) sugar
2 tablespoons mustard seeds
1½ teaspoons turmeric
4 cups (1 liter) cider vinegar
2 cups (500 ml) water

1. Mix together the onions, cabbage, tomatoes, green and red peppers in a large bowl. Sprinkle on the salt and allow to stand overnight.
2. Rinse the vegetables and drain well. Put into a large saucepan.
3. Mix together the sugar, mustard seeds, turmeric, cider vinegar and water in a saucepan. Heat, stirring constantly, until the sugar has dissolved.
4. Pour the vinegar mixture over the vegetables and bring to a boil. Reduce heat and simmer for three minutes.
5. Pour into warm sterilized jars and cover with two layers of wax paper and one layer of aluminum foil. Tie securely with string.
6. Keep for a few days before eating.

Crisp Pickle Slices

4 lb (2 kg) medium cucumbers
3 medium white onions, chopped
1 green pepper, chopped
2 cloves garlic
⅓ cup coarse salt

2½ cups sugar
1½ cups (375 ml) cider vinegar
1 teaspoon turmeric
1 teaspoon celery seeds
1½ tablespoons mustard seeds

1. Slice the cucumbers thinly. Do not peel.
2. Put the cucumbers in a large bowl with the onions, pepper and whole garlic. Sprinkle on the salt and cover with crushed ice. Allow to stand for four hours. Drain well.
3. Put the cucumber mixture into a large saucepan.
4. Mix together the sugar, vinegar, turmeric, celery seeds and mustard seeds. Pour over the cucumber mixture.
5. Bring to a boil, stirring constantly.
6. Pour into warm sterilized jars. Seal immediately.

Dilled Carrot Sticks

6 lb (3 kg) young carrots
24 large sprigs dill
6 cloves garlic, peeled
2½ tablespoons mixed pickling spices

⅓ cup salt
1 cup (250 ml) cider vinegar
6 cups (1½ liters) water

1. Peel the carrots and cut into 2-inch (5-cm) long sticks.
2. Cook in boiling water until almost tender. Drain.
3. Place two sprigs of dill on the bottom of each of six sterilized half-quart jars.
4. Pack the carrots in the jars.
5. Put one garlic clove in each jar.
6. Put pickling spices and remaining dill on top.
7. Heat together salt, vinegar and water to the boiling point.
8. Fill each jar to overflowing, cover and seal.
9. Keep for at least three weeks before using.

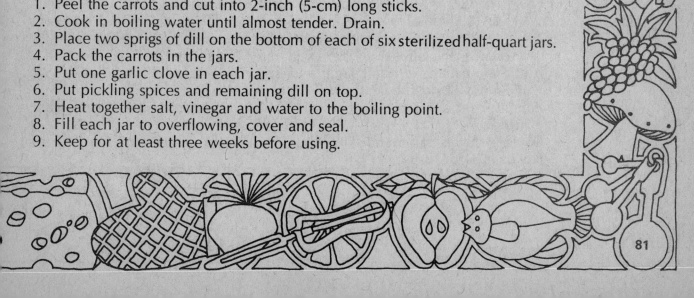

Pickled Red Peppers

6 large red peppers, seeded and halved lengthwise
4 cups (1 liter) white wine vinegar
½ teaspoon salt

10 black peppercorns
5 parsley sprigs
1 thyme spray
1 bay leaf
⅓ cup (85 ml) olive oil

1. Put the peppers, skin sides up, under a hot broiler for about six minutes or until the skins are black and charred. Remove from the broiler and rub off the charred skin.
2. Cut the peppers into slices and put them into warm sterilized jars.
3. Mix together the vinegar, salt and peppercorns in a saucepan.
4. Tie together the parsley, thyme and bay leaf and add to the vinegar mixture. Bring to a boil.
5. Remove from heat and strain in the jars.
6. When cool, pour equal amounts of olive oil into each jar.
7. Cover and put in a cool, dark place.

Beet Pickle

7 medium beets, raw
cold water
1½ cups (375 ml) wine vinegar
1¼ tablespoons dry mustard
½ teaspoon salt
1 cup sugar
2 medium onions, sliced
2½ teaspoons dill seeds

1. Wash the beets well and put into a saucepan with enough cold water to cover. Bring to a boil and cook until the beets are tender. Drain, reserving 1¼ cups (300 ml) of the cooking liquid. When the beets are cool, cut off the top and bottom and gently slip off the skins. Slice and set aside.
2. Mix together the vinegar and reserved liquid in a saucepan. Bring to a boil.
3. Add the mustard, salt and sugar and, stirring constantly, bring back to a boil. Remove from the heat.
4. Put the beet slices in warm sterilized jars and pour on the hot vinegar mixture.
5. Cover with wax paper and screw tops. Store in the refrigerator. Keep for a few days before using.

Apple and Tomato Pickle

2 lb (1 kg) apples
6 lb (3 kg) tomatoes
2 medium onions
2½ tablespoons mustard seeds
4 tablespoons ground ginger

4 tablespoons coarse salt
10 peppercorns
5 cups (1¼ liters) vinegar
2½ cups brown sugar

1. Peel the apples and tomatoes and cut into chunks.
2. Peel the onions and chop finely.
3. Mix together the apples, tomatoes and onions with the mustard seeds, ginger, salt, peppercorns and vinegar.
4. Bring to a boil. Reduce heat, cover and simmer until the apples soften.
5. Add the sugar and stir until sugar is dissolved.
6. Continue to simmer until all the ingredients are reduced to a pulp. Stir well.
7. Remove from the heat and cool.
8. When cool, pour into jars. When cold, cover with two layers of wax paper and one layer of aluminum foil. Tie securely with string.
9. May be used in a few days.

Cauliflower and Tomato Pickle

2 medium cauliflowers, cut
   into flowerets
1½ lb (750 g) tomatoes,
   quartered
5 medium onions, chopped
1 medium cucumber,
   chopped
⅔ cup coarse salt

1 teaspoon dry mustard
¾ teaspoon ground ginger
1¼ teaspoons black pepper
1¼ cups brown sugar
1 teaspoon pickling spice
2½ cups (625 ml) white
   vinegar

1. Put the vegetables in layers in a deep dish sprinkling the salt between the layers. Cover with cold water, put on a lid and allow to stand overnight.
2. Drain the vegetables and rinse well under cold running water. Drain well.
3. Put the vegetables in a large saucepan and add the mustard, ginger, pepper, sugar and pickling spice.
4. Pour on the vinegar and bring to a boil, stirring constantly. Reduce heat and simmer for 20 minutes or until the vegetables are tender but firm.
5. Spoon the vegetables into warm sterilized jars and fill with the liquid.
6. Cover with two layers of wax paper and one layer of aluminum foil. Tie securely with string.
7. Keep for a week before using.

Pickled Beans

1½ teaspoons salt
4 cups (1 liter) white wine vinegar
½ cup sugar
3 cloves garlic, peeled

2 bay leaves
2 medium onions, sliced
10 black peppercorns
2 teaspoons dill seeds
2 lb (1 kg) fresh green beans

1. Mix together one teaspoon salt, the vinegar, sugar, garlic, bay leaves, onions, peppercorns and dill seeds in a saucepan. Bring to a boil. Reduce heat and simmer for ½ hour over a low heat.
2. Put the beans in a saucepan of boiling water with the remaining ½ teaspoon salt and cook for five minutes.
3. Drain the beans and put them upright into warm sterilized jars.
4. Strain the liquid and pour over the beans up to the tops of the jars. Seal and store in a cool dark place.

Pickled Cucumbers

2 lb (1 kg) young cucumbers
5 cups (1¼ liters) water
⅔ cup cooking salt
¼ cup sugar
5 cups (1¼ liters) spiced vinegar (see index)
dried bay leaves

1. Wipe the cucumbers with a damp cloth. Quarter them lengthwise. (Do not peel.)
2. Boil together the water and salt. Cool.
3. Put the cucumbers in the brine and allow to stand for 24 hours.
4. Mix the sugar in the spiced vinegar until it is dissolved.
5. Remove the cucumbers from the brine, rinse in cold water and drain thoroughly. Set aside for two hours to dry.
6. Put the dry cucumbers in jars and fill with spiced vinegar ensuring that the vinegar covers the top of the cucumbers by at least ½ inch (one cm).
7. Put a bay leaf on the top of the cucumbers in each jar.
8. Cover the jars first with two layers of wax paper, then one layer of aluminum foil. Tie securely.
9. Keep for three weeks before using.

Corn Pickle

1 medium cucumber, peeled	2½ tablespoons coarse salt
3 medium onions, peeled	½ teaspoon black pepper
1 medium green pepper, seeded	1¼ cups (300 ml) cider vinegar
¾ lb (375 g) tomatoes, peeled and seeded	⅔ cup (165 ml) water
2 lb (1 kg) corn kernels	½ teaspoon turmeric
1 cup sugar	1¼ teaspoons dry mustard

1. Cut the cucumber, onions, green pepper and tomatoes into cubes.
2. Put all the ingredients except the tomatoes into a large saucepan. Bring to a boil, stirring constantly. Boil for five minutes.
3. Cover the saucepan and simmer for one hour.
4. Add the tomatoes and cook for another five minutes.
5. Pour into warm sterilized jars and cover with two layers of wax paper and one layer of aluminum foil. Tie securely with string.
6. Keep for about a month before using.

Mixed Pickles

1 lb (500 g) scallions
1 lb (500 g) cauliflower
1 large cucumber
2 tablespoons coarse salt
6 cups (1½ liters) spiced vinegar (see index)

1. Peel the scallions and cut the cauliflower into flowerets. Peel the cucumber and cut it into cubes.
2. Put the scallions, cauliflower and cucumber on a dish and sprinkle with the 2½ tablespoons of salt. Allow to stand overnight.
3. Strain off the salt and put the vegetables into a glass jar (or jars) in layers.
4. Fill with cold spiced vinegar covering the vegetables with at least ½ inch (one cm) at the top.
5. Cover the jar with two layers of wax paper and one layer of aluminum foil then tie securely.
6. Keep for two to three months before using.

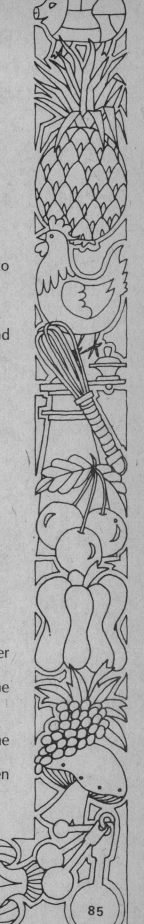

Sweet Pickled Scallions

2 lb (1 kg) scallions
8 cups (2 liters) water
1½ cups coarse salt
5 cups (1½ liters) spiced
   vinegar (see index)
½ cup sugar

1. Peel the scallions.
2. Boil the water with the salt and allow to cool.
3. Pour half the brine over the scallions and allow to stand for two days. Drain.
4. Pour on the remaining brine and allow to stand for another two days.
5. Drain and rinse the scallions.
6. Put the scallions into a saucepan with the spiced vinegar and the sugar. Bring to a boil. Reduce heat and simmer for ten minutes.
7. Pour the scallions and vinegar into jars.
8. Cover first with two layers of wax paper, then one layer of aluminum foil. When cool, tie securely.
9. Keep for three weeks before using.

Spiced Vinegar

1 oz (30 g) peppercorns
⅓ oz (10 g) blade mace
⅓ oz (10 g) cloves
6 bay leaves
½ oz (15 g) crushed fresh
   ginger

2½ teaspoons mustard seeds
⅓ oz (10 g) whole allspice
⅓ oz (10 g) cinnamon stick
2 teaspoons celery seeds
1¼ tablespoons salt
4 cups (1 liter) malt vinegar

1. Mix together all the spices and salt in a saucepan.
2. Add ½ cup of vinegar and bring to a boil.
3. Boil for two minutes.
4. Add the remaining vinegar and boil for another three minutes.
5. Strain and cool.

Pickled Mushrooms

1 lb (500 g) button mushrooms	1 teaspoon coarse salt
2½ cups (625 ml) white vinegar	½ teaspoon white pepper
	small piece of fresh root ginger
	1 medium onion, sliced

1. Wipe the mushrooms with a damp cloth.
2. Put the mushrooms into a saucepan with the vinegar, salt, pepper, ginger and onion. (If the vinegar does not cover the mushrooms, add a little more.)
3. Bring to a boil. Reduce heat and simmer until the mushrooms are tender.
4. Lift the mushrooms out and place in warm jars.
5. Pour the hot vinegar over the mushrooms making sure that the vinegar covers the mushrooms by at least ½ inch (one cm).
6. Cover the jars with two layers of wax paper, then one layer of aluminum foil. Tie securely.
7. May be eaten in a few days.

Pickled Red Cabbage

3 lb (1½ kg) red cabbage
5 tablespoons coarse salt
3½ cups (875 ml) cold spiced
    vinegar (see index)

1. Remove the outer leaves from the cabbage. Wash the cabbage under cold running water then cut it into quarters. Cut into shreds.
2. Spread the cabbage out on a dish and sprinkle with five tablespoons salt. Allow to stand overnight.
3. Put the cabbage into a colander and allow to drain thoroughly.
4. Put the cabbage into glass jars and cover with the spiced vinegar. Allow to stand overnight.
5. Top up the jars with vinegar so that the cabbage is completely covered with the vinegar.
6. Put two layers of wax paper, then one layer of aluminum foil on top of the jar and tie securely.
7. Keep for two weeks before using.

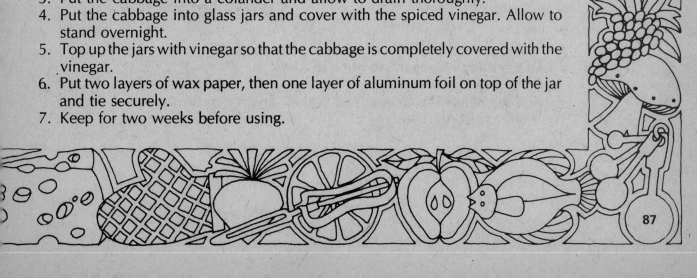

Pickled Scallions

2 lb (1 kg) scallions
4 tablespoons coarse salt
5 cups (1¼ liters) spiced
   vinegar (see index)

1. Peel the scallions and put them on a shallow dish.
2. Sprinkle with the four tablespoons salt and allow to stand overnight.
3. Put the scallions in a colander and allow to drain thoroughly.
4. Pack into jars arranging so that there are no large spaces.
5. Fill the jars with spiced vinegar making sure that there is at least ½ inch (one cm) of vinegar covering the top of the scallions.
6. Put two layers of wax paper then one layer of aluminum foil on the top of the jars and tie securely.
7. Keep for four weeks before using.

Cucumber and Apple Pickle

3 medium cucumbers, sliced
3 lb (1½ kg) red apples, cored
   and sliced
5 cups (1¼ liters) water
¾ cup (185 ml) lemon juice

5 tablespoons coarse salt
2½ cups brown sugar
3¾ cups (875 ml) cider
3 ¾ cups (875 ml) vinegar

1. Put the cucumbers and apples in a large bowl.
2. Mix together the water, lemon juice and salt and pour over the cucumbers and apples. Set aside for four hours.
3. Drain and rinse in cold water.
4. Mix together the sugar, cider and vinegar in a saucepan.
5. Bring to a boil, then add the cucumbers and apples. Simmer for three minutes.
6. Put the cucumbers and apples into sterilised jars and pour the liquid over until overflowing.
7. Cover with two layers of wax paper, then one layer of aluminum foil. Tie securely with string.
8. May be eaten in a few days.

Sweet Mustard Pickle

1 medium marrow
1 medium cauliflower
1 medium cucumber
1 lb (500 g) onions
1 lb (500 g) green beans
2 tablespoons coarse salt
⅓ cup dry mustard

2½ tablespoons ground turmeric
2 tablespoons ground ginger
2½ tablespoons ground nutmeg
1¼ cups sugar
½ cup plain flour
5 cups (1¼ liters) vinegar

1. Chop the vegetables into small cubes and put into a dish.
2. Sprinkle the salt over the vegetables, then add enough water to cover. Allow to stand overnight, then drain off the water.
3. Mix together the mustard, turmeric, ginger, nutmeg, sugar and flour. Add a little vinegar to make a smooth paste.
4. Put the drained vegetables into a saucepan and pour on the remaining vinegar. Bring to a boil. Reduce heat and simmer for about ten minutes.
5. Spoon some of the hot vinegar from the vegetables into the flour and spice mixture and stir well. Pour back into the sauce and boil for about ten minutes, stirring constantly until smooth and thick.
6. Pour the vegetables while still hot into jars.
7. Cover with two layers of wax paper and then one layer of aluminum foil. When cool, tie securely.
8. May be used in a few days.

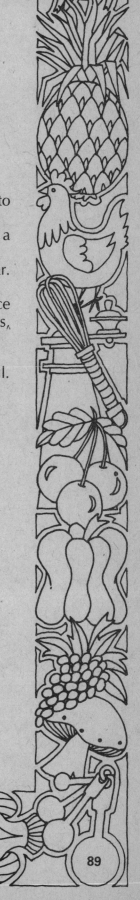

Chow-Chow

1 lb (500 g) cucumbers, chopped
1 lb (500 g) green tomatoes, sliced
1 lb (500 g) onions, sliced
1 lb (500 g) scallions, peeled
1 lb (500 g) cauliflower, cut into flowerets
1 lb (500 g) celery, chopped

3 tablespoons coarse salt
10 cups (2½ liters) cold water
6 tablespoons plain flour
2 tablespoons ground turmeric
1 cup sugar
5 cups (1¼ liters) spiced vinegar (see index)

1. Put the prepared vegetables into a large saucepan.
2. Dissolve the salt in the water and pour over the vegetables. Cover and set aside for 24 hours.
3. Bring the vegetables and the brine to a boil. Drain and keep warm.
4. Mix together the flour, mustard, turmeric and sugar. Add a little of the vinegar to make a smooth paste.
5. In the top of a double boiler, heat the vinegar.
6. Slowly add the paste, stirring constantly. Cook, continuing to stir, until thick and smooth.
7. Add to the hot vegetables and cook for 15 minutes.
8. Pour the chow-chow into warm jars.
9. Cover first with two layers of wax paper, then one layer of aluminum foil. When cool, tie securely.
10. May be eaten in a few days.

Spiced Sweet Pickled Cucumber

4 lb (2 kg) large cucumbers
coarse salt
water
1 teaspoon alum
6 cups (1½ liters) white malt
vinegar

3 lb (1½ kg) sugar
2½ oz (75 g) mixed pickling
spices
1 inch (2½ cm) cinnamon
stick

1. Wipe the cucumbers with a damp cloth. Cut them into quarters lengthwise, then into chunks. Put them into an earthenware bowl.
2. Pour enough brine over the cucumbers to cover them. (Make the brine by mixing 3 tablespoons of salt with 2½ cups/½ liter of water). Add the alum.
3. Cover and set aside for three days.
4. Drain and rinse well with cold water.
5. Put the cucumbers into a saucepan with 2½ cups vinegar. Add water if the vinegar does not quite cover the cucumbers.
6. Bring to a boil. Reduce the heat and simmer for about half an hour or until tender.
7. Drain the cucumbers and put into an earthenware bowl.
8. Put the remaining vinegar into a saucepan with the sugar. Mix in the pickling spices and the cinnamon stick tied in a piece of muslin. Boil for five minutes.
9. Pour the hot spiced vinegar over the cucumbers and set aside for 24 hours.
10. Strain the vinegar off the cucumbers and put in a saucepan. Bring back to a boil, then pour back over the cucumbers. Set aside for another 24 hours.
11. Repeat step 10.
12. Strain off the vinegar and pack the cucumbers into warm jars.
13. Boil the vinegar rapidly until it is reduced by about a third. Pour over the cucumbers.
14. When cool, cover the jars first with two layers of wax paper, then a layer of aluminum foil. Tie securely.
15. May be eaten in a few days.

Pickled Watermelon Rind

4 lb (2 kg) watermelon rind
8 cups sugar
4 cups (1 liter) cider vinegar
4 cups (1 liter) water
2 oranges

2 lemons
4 sticks cinnamon
1 tablespoon whole cloves
2 tablespoons whole allspice

1. Scrape off any pink flesh from the rind. Cut into 1-inch (2½-cm) squares.
2. Cover with cold, salted water (¼ cup salt for 4 cups water) and allow to stand overnight. Drain.
3. Put the watermelon rind in a large saucepan and cover with cold water. Simmer for 30 minutes or until just tender. Drain again.
4. Mix together the sugar, vinegar and water in a large saucepan. Heat, stirring constantly, until the sugar dissolves.
5. Cut the oranges and lemons into thin slices, remove the pips and add the fruit to the sugar mixture.
6. Tie the cinnamon, cloves and allspice in a piece of muslin and place in the saucepan.
7. Bring the mixture to a boil.
8. Add the watermelon rind and cook for 1½ to 2 hours or until the rind is translucent and the juices syrupy.
9. Put into warm sterilized jars and seal.

Tomato Pickle

6 lb (3 kg) tomatoes, peeled
5 tablespoons salt
2 lb (1 kg) onions
1¼ tablespoons cloves
1¼ tablespoons mustard seeds

2 teaspoons pepper
4 lb (2 kg) sugar
⅔ cup (165 ml) treacle
4 cups (1 liter) vinegar

1. Slice the tomatoes and sprinkle with the salt. Allow to stand overnight. Strain.
2. Peel and slice the onions and put into a large saucepan with the remaining ingredients.
3. Cook over a low heat until the sugar is dissolved.
4. Bring to a boil. Reduce heat and cook until the onions are tender.
5. Add the tomatoes and cook of another ½ hour.
6. Pour into warm sterilized jars and cover with two layers of wax paper and one layer of aluminum foil. Tie securely with string.

Marrow Pickle

1 large vegetable marrow,
 peeled, seeded and diced
1 lb (500 g) onions, chopped
3 tablespoons salt
1½ tablespoons ground ginger
1½ tablespoons turmeric

1½ teaspoons cloves
5 green chillis, halved
 lengthwise, seeds removed
10 peppercorns
2 cups brown sugar
8 cups (2 litres) malt vinegar

1. Put the marrow and onions in a bowl in layers, sprinkling salt between the layers. Cover and allow to stand overnight. Drain well.
2. Mix together the ginger, turmeric, cloves, chillies, peppercorns, sugar and vinegar. Heat, stirring constantly, until sugar dissolves. Then bring to a boil. Reduce heat and simmer for ½ hour.
3. Stir in the marrow and onions and return to a boil. Reduce heat and simmer for 1½ hours or until the mixture is thick.
4. Pour into warm sterilized jars and cover with two layers of wax paper and one layer of aluminum foil. Tie securely with string.

Orange Pickle

7 oranges
1 teaspoon salt
1 lb (500 g) sugar
3 tablespoons corn syrup
¾ cup (185 ml) malt vinegar
½ cup (125 ml) water

seeds of 5 cardamoms
8 black peppercorns, crushed
¾ teaspoon ground cinnamon
¼ teaspoon ground allspice
10 cloves

1. Place the oranges and salt in a large saucepan and cover with cold water. Bring to a boil. Reduce heat and simmer for about one hour or until the oranges are tender.
2. Drain the oranges and allow to cool.
3. Mix together the remaining ingredients in a saucepan and bring to a boil, stirring constantly. Reduce heat and simmer for ten minutes. Remove from heat and cool.
4. Cut the cooled oranges into thin slices.
5. Pour the cooled vinegar mixture through a strainer.
6. Put the orange slices and strained liquid into a saucepan and bring to a boil. Reduce heat and simmer for ½ hour.
7. Remove from heat and allow to stand for five minutes.
8. Spoon into warm sterilized jars and cover with two layers of wax paper and one layer of aluminum foil.
9. Keep for three weeks before using.

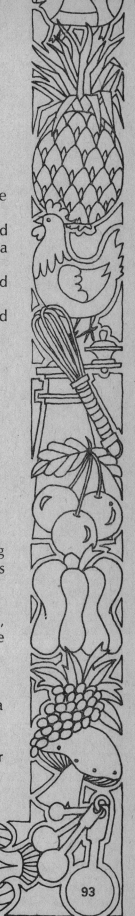

Piccalilli

1 medium cucumber, peeled and cubed
1 lb (500 g) cauliflower, cut into flowerets
1 lb (500 g) scallion, peeled and sliced
1 lb (500 g) green tomatoes, sliced
1 green pepper, seeded and chopped

1 lb (500 g) shredded cabbage
1 lb (500 g) coarse salt
4 cups (1 liter) vinegar
1¼ tablespoons turmeric
1¼ tablespoons dry mustard
1¼ tablespoons ground ginger
2 cloves garlic, minced
¾ cup sugar
4 tablespoons cornstarch

1. Spread the vegetables on a large dish and sprinkle with the salt. Allow to stand overnight. Drain and rinse well in cold water.
2. Put all but ¼ cup of the vinegar into a large saucepan with the turmeric, mustard, ginger, garlic and sugar. Bring to a boil.
3. Add the vegetables and simmer until the vegetables are still just crisp.
4. Mix the cornstarch with the remaining vinegar. Add to the vegetables and mix well.
5. Boil for three minutes, stirring constantly.
6. Spoon into warm sterilized jars and cover with two layers of wax paper and one layer of aluminum foil. Tie securely with string.
7. Keep for a couple of weeks before using.

Index